**Nuala S. White** MSc; pgDip.Couns; mBACP; Fellow CIPD

I'm Nuala, Lulu and a wayshower.

I've always been passionate about the inner child in us all. Starting with myself as Lulu in early childhood learning to navigate the massive works of the heart through all the programming and beliefs and limitations given by parents, big people and life.

A personal development and change expert since 1983, when my world changed in a flash as I discovered there was a 'ME'. A me who could choose who to be and how to be! And so the journey began.

I have trained and delivered countless programmes as a personal development facilitator and corporate change Leader and learning consultant. A qualified psychotherapist, and rapid change coach in numerous modalities. The essence is 'Being With' – that pure space that opens through the deepest listening. I call on divine light and love as the powerful healers that free myself and others, yet fully grounded in the real ordinary and extraordinary lives I'm blessed to help.

All my life's experience brought together to serve the work of igniting your inner child in service to your now life.

Life and family traumas brought me sickness and chronic disease. I know the conflicts within family when we cannot change the dynamic or clear the pain that brings broken doors and walls and hearts. And living surrounded by Aspergers in the home has not been an easy ride.

My greatest life challenge came when beloved husband had a near fatal brain haemorrhage in 2013. Every skill in my tool bag and every shred of inner strength empowered Don's rehabilitation from profound disability back to walking, talking, driving, working and LIVING!

Now stepping into my light with self love and an honouring of the shadows, my life and family have been transformed. Miracle moments occur almost every day. We are healing.

My life and work are a pure joy, full of wonder and challenge, light and shade, and a yellow brick road.

I'll follow the path given clearly to me by God…the Spirit in me, wherever it may lead...

Lulu is the first of a series of books… "When the Troubles began. The growing-up years"; "Poetry of life"; and workbooks.

My MSC in Asperger's. 'Finding the positive' is published.

If you would like to contact me please do. I'm so keen to know how your own inner child responds.

Nualaswhite@gmail.com. Learning-for-Living.com Facebook 'Lulu and me and you'.

Dedicated to my most loving Mammy Susan…Susie.
Kindest gentlest soul who sacrificed herself for us.

And Margaret, my perfect sister, who went to heaven too young.

Nuala Susan White

# LULU...
# RE-MEMBER YOUR HEART

AUSTIN MACAULEY PUBLISHERS™

LONDON · CAMBRIDGE · NEW YORK · SHARJAH

A CIP catalogue record for this title is available from the British Library.

ISBN 9781528983679 (Paperback)
ISBN 9781528983686 (ePub e-book)

www.austinmacauley.com

First Published (2020)
Austin Macauley Publishers Ltd
25 Canada Square
Canary Wharf
London
E14 5LQ

# Acknowledgements

With deep loving gratitude to my lifetime partner, Don White, for his endless willingness to support and hold through the dark and light times.

To my own children, Tara and Danny, for teaching me so much as I learned to love me and parent myself alongside them.

To the many beautiful troubled souls who have dared to knock my door and ask for help and dared to open up to themselves and release it all. You inspire me always to be a worthy companion.

To my sisters and brothers, who each have their own childhood still inside, and their own memories. This carries only love for us all.

And thanks to my illustrator, the artist Clare Kelly, who has said:
I found myself being taken hand in hand through the pages and brought to rediscover the younger Clare that still dwells within. The wee Clare whose heart was always so full of love for everyone and everything but whose light had dimmed somewhat over the years but was rekindling again. I brought her out to play as I resiliently allowed myself to heal whilst producing the paintings and drawings for this beautiful book.

'Polishing' my heart as I went…
I was steadily reclaiming the LULU in ME!
It has been an absolute delight to have had the opportunity to illustrate LULU. To me this is a manuscript that reminds us that no matter what our experiences as children were or are that we were and are LOVE.
May WE find that inner PEACE in our wonderful hearts, spirit and souls again.
I sincerely HOPE and TRUST that LULU will FLY off the bookshelves into the hands and hearts of people of all ages for them too to GROW and HEAL.
Thank you Nuala/LULU for this very special gift from your child spirit to ours with LOVE.
Clare Kelly B.A..

# Table of Contents

# Lost heart

Where did you lose your heart dear child
Where did you leave your heart?
What was that pain that terror that spear
that pierced you so deeply you can't even weep?
For tears need to flow somewhere in your deep.

But icicles formed as your ice age began
when the decision was made to be frozen in time.
Your iceberg whose tip warns don't come too close
What lies beneath, a sea of reproach,
A cold mountain of feeling. Do not approach.

But why did you lose your heart dear child
Why did you leave your heart?
Abandoned locked up, chained in, ignored.
Were the memories too harsh? This living too sore?
So for your own safety you silenced its roars.

For the pain so real, the habit so strong
Cover up, pretend, play along, give more.
From the empty chalice can someone please see
my empty, poor – someone please… rescue me!
Can someone else quench this thirst, give heat to the ice, melt this
aching heart
Bring it back to life?

And what if you opened your heart dear child
What if you reclaim your heart?
Is the fear too great to save your own life?

What will become me if I melt and dissolve?
What flood will wash me away, leave but silt and mud?
Destroy all in its path. I would be no more.
They may not survive when I'm not there to shore –
up – our lives, our needs, our pain, our sore
broken hearts, that I've held on the shore.

But what if you shine again dear child?
What if your spark caught fire?
Let the ice melt, breathe God to your core.
Let the sun melt your frozen, Let the light shine once more.
And Channel the drip the deluge the flood
Of rage and grief and wasted love?
To fill your own chalice in mercy and love.

You came here as love, flowing, crystal clear.
and yes life brought its horrors, its troubles is sludge.
Please swim in the waters, splash in the mud.
Set them free to float on their own life force, find their own boat.
Cry your own tears, let them cry theirs.
Give the gift of freedom to your heart and theirs.

Re Member your heart dear child
Hold her close, let her cry
Let her know you will hold her and leave her no more.

# Foreword

One little girl's life of love and fear and freedom…

Maybe this book is for big grown-up people like you, first, who have somehow decided to forget the big beautiful child's heart that still beats inside you.

You came into this world as LOVE. A love that can never be extinguished. A pure love that restores and heals everything in its path.

When big people like you remember and learn to listen and feel again, properly feel, your hearts can shine out, and you can really love yourself. Then, you have a beautiful gift that lets others shine out too.

And then, also for your children, who are all busy being themselves and most likely trying to work out how to be or who to love in this world, need someone bigger to make sure they feel safe enough to love that big heart inside themselves.

When you dare to look inside, all your incredible memories and feelings can bubble up in your senses, forgotten and now, remembered again. All the ones you big people have learned to judge as good and bad. Then you will feel your own big heart alive and well and longing to be seen, loved and healed by you, when you let yourself out to play.

Your big heart will be ready to hear and the children will know when you are there with them, because then, they will tell you. They will show you all their dreams, confusion and fears because you will have shown them by being real again.

And we can be the parent to that child inside ourselves, who is waiting to be heard, to be held and loved. It is never too late to give ourselves the love we needed, and be the parent we always wanted.

Lulu came through at night to awaken and record the memories of a time before the world shaped her, before she got tangled in the tricky business of growing up. Mostly it seems she wanted to be seen in all her innocence.

Like we all do. She came back to be re-membered as the pure innocent spark who was too little to make sense of the world she came into and to finally let go of fear. And as these memories, stories were re-membered then she was healed and free to be herself again, unafraid and unashamed, an adult ready to live and love and spread it around.
She has finally been allowed to go out and play.

Little Lulu calls you to come out to play and allow your own early childhood the space it has needed to breathe the memories, to be understood. The answers to yourself are waiting there. None of it was your fault. You did nothing wrong! That great big heart of love inside YOU is beautiful and perfect and will never leave you, no matter how grown up and important you become.

Please, Re-member your heart!

# Lulu

Lulu was a wee bundle of life.

Lulu was the 'baby' and as she watched her nine big sisters and brothers being very big and busy, she just seemed to disappear into her own wee, enormous world.

She seemed to find herself in all sorts of situations as she found her way exploring and simply being in the big world!

She never understood or even asked how come things happened or what she did. Little ones don't you know! Everything just pours in and out again, every sound and sight, taste and smell and feeling. Lulu was led by this incredible big heart full of life and opportunities.

She was often told off for her adventures, though many she kept inside her heart, and it was only many, many years later that she finally began to love herself and all that love inside her.

There were lots of things that Lulu liked and there were lots of things that she didn't like at all.

Lulu really didn't like the nit comb because of her great big mass of tangly, curly fair hair. She used to get this used a lot, and she objected loudly in tears every time.

She didn't like having to wear a liberty bodice all summer long. It stuck out from under her summer dress and was itchy.

She didn't like everybody shouting and fighting, and she didn't like thunder and lightning because she really believed she would die.

She didn't like escalators, those moving staircases that they put in big shops because she always thought she would fall off. She didn't like the green medicine and she didn't like the dark. She was terrified of the big black hoover and its roar as the others chased her round the floor with it.

And she would run all the way home when the tractor was around the pavilion field.

Lulu really, really liked sweets, even though that meant she had to go to the dentist a lot and she really, really did not like the dentists! Ever since the day he pushed her into the chair and threatened to tie her up, because she didn't like the big black gas mask going over her face.

She really, really liked…no, loved, being at the shore especially when the tide was in and when the wash from the big ships crashed in and she got wet.

She really liked when everyone gathered in the big upstairs sitting room at night to watch Roy Rodgers and the Lone Ranger and she could snuggle up on the floor and smell the big old sofa.

And Lulu loved it when the big ones picked her up and gave her a burly, where they spun her round and round in circles until she was dizzy and sick and her chest got wheezy again.

And she really liked hearing Mammy sing the hundreds of songs she knew when she was working in the kitchen.

Mostly, Lulu just was, and she still just is…herself!

It's just that Lulu couldn't help but follow her heart and be herself. And even though the big ones always told her she was wrong - probably because they were scared - now more than ever, she knows it is worth following your heart instead of fear.

It's strange how people bigger than us can make us feel scared when the feeling doesn't really belong to us, and we don't feel that, but because they are scared, they kind of pass that on. That can get very confusing because it can then feel so real that we don't know whether to listen to our own hearts or not. At times like those, it would be really good if we could just talk about that mixed up confusion, without anyone else telling us what they think it should be like. Like sorting shells at the shore, we could lay them all out in ones that feel right and smell good, and ones that don't seem to fit or look dull and wrong somehow. Then, we could choose.

# Breathing

Lulu was sick a lot. From very early on, she found breathing a problem. Daddy always blamed her when she got sick and couldn't breathe. He said it was because she had been rolling in the long grass of the second shore field or down the railway embankment. But she couldn't help herself. Rolling down the big bank was just pure joy and freed her whole body with laughter, giggles and delight. And making forts in the second shore field, where the grass was bigger than her was just perfect. Some days, it was hard to find a spot that wasn't already flattened or where couples would lie, kiss and hug. They were very funny, but they didn't like us kids being anywhere near them. The smell of the long grass was good enough to eat and it was so warm and safe inside the tall grass walls that she laid flat around the edges of her very own den.

When she was sick, Mammy got horrible yellow green medicine from the doctors, and what a fuss Lulu kicked up when she had to swallow the slimy goo that stuck in her throat.

Mammy got honey to help too, but Lulu didn't like that either. Poor Mum was probably at her wits end with worry, in case Lulu would stop breathing and die.

She had to take Lulu to the hospital a lot, all the way to Belfast on the bus, and the best bit was that she got to be with Mammy, just me and her.

We nearly always got a cup of tea and a bun on those days and when she took me to the doctors down the street. Lulu always remembered getting a great big cream bun, and it felt like a very special, private time with each other. The bigger ones probably never got that time where they felt like they were the only one in the world who mattered. Maybe this was another really good reason for getting sick so often?

When Lulu grew up and had her own children, she carried on the tradition of tea and buns on the way home from the doctors. And all those precious memories of Mammy's love came flooding back in, alive again.

Mammy was always working, always in the kitchen, washing all the clothes for all the boys, ironing and cooking the spuds for dinner.

The hospital gave Lulu special exercises to do and a special pillow for bed.

*'Thin as a rake, wide as a gate, long as a pole, short as a roll. Big as a house, small as a mouse'.*

This was to help open her airways and it was fun to do with a big sister, as she stretched over the bed, head on the floor.

Imagine your airways getting shut! Like when cars get into a traffic jam and they are all desperate to get somewhere and all the fumes invisibly spread into all the cars and the traffic can go nowhere until it gets unstuck… I suppose Lulu somehow got stuck in a traffic jam inside, trying to make sense of everything going on around her. Everyone does sometimes. Do you?

The big ones sometimes thought it was really funny to jump on Lulu when she was in bed sick.

They would pull all the covers over her head and pin her down inside so she couldn't breathe at all. Lulu didn't like this! She used to think she was going to die. They only seemed to let go when Lulu was on her last breath.

She didn't understand why they had to do this to her, but now she knows they were all just up to mischief, doing what they could to have fun. Ten growing up ones all in the one house where they had to stay quiet a lot of the time, probably meant everyone felt squashed and unable to breathe properly, in one way or another.

And now, Lulu knows, because some of them told her much later that they were jealous. Jealous of the 'baby' of the family, who they thought got more love than they did. Each and everyone just wanted to know they were loved.

That's a feeling we all pretend not to have, I think, so we hide it under all the things we do and say. It seems being jealous is made into a very bad or dirty feeling that we aren't supposed to have. But when you think about it, it's just another way of our heart telling us what we want or need that is lacking, and what we want more for ourselves. Our feelings always have something to tell us. Lulu knows that we all just want to be loved and that no matter what, she always will believe we are good enough exactly how we are. We are all perfect hearts of love.

# Being Sick

When Lulu was sick and had to stay home from school in bed, the house was very, very quiet. Thirty-six stairs up all alone in the attic bedroom she shared with her big sisters, Lulu listened for every sound.

Sometimes, she just used to lie listening to her chest squeaking away to her like a chatterbox. Sometimes, she couldn't resist picking the little soft threads that made up the pattern on the cover of the top blanket, until she realised lots of big gaps appeared out of nowhere. Mammy was never very happy about this. But the other blankets were too heavy and stiff and Lulu just loved the soft velvety feeling as she plucked and plucked.

She could tell the time by the bell of the big school across the field when all the chatter and din of morning break time in the playground carried across and into the bedroom.

She knew when the Angelus bells of the chapel rang that it was twelve o'clock. Then she knew it would be school lunchtime when it was if hundreds of children were out at a party because of all the laughing, shouting and just noise.

She listened for everything and the biggest sound she waited to hear was when Daddy would come home for dinner at two o'clock.

First, the car would pull up at the house, then the footsteps up the path. The front door would open and close, and then silence as he went into the kitchen.

Lulu's breathing was the worst at this time, because she had to hold her breath to try and figure out if everything was going to be okay or if Daddy was going to be angry or if Mammy was going to be upset.

So, she listened and listened, even though her wheezy chest made such a loud noise against her beating heart, and sometimes, she tiptoed out onto the top landing to make sure she could hear. Sshh.

The radio being switched on, the dinner noise of plates and dishes, the coal being shovelled onto the fire, the radio crackled with old Irish fiddles or horse racing shouted out as the winner came home first. And then all would be silent again so she knew Daddy had gone to his wee chair by the fire to sleep.

Lulu didn't know why then but now, she does. This being 'afraid feeling' that still comes out of nowhere even when she is all grown-up.

That feeling that seems to block out our heart and stop us breathing as we wait for some unknown bad thing to happen. They call that a special word nowadays but all Lulu knew then, was how it felt when she held her breath ready for something not nice that might not even happen.

Some days, Lulu dared to or needed to find out what was happening down in the kitchen when Daddy was in for dinner or she was hungry.

So, she would come down very quietly, always finding a way to miss the creaky stairs, every single one remembered, and quietly creep into the kitchen.

Sometimes, everything was okay and Daddy would let her have the skin of his fried herrings that she just loved.

Mammy always had soup or stew ready.

But sometimes, it all felt wrong down there and Lulu and even Mammy seemed to tiptoe about so as not to disturb or annoy Daddy.

One of these days, the quiet was louder than ever and after waiting a long time trying to figure out what was happening, Lulu tiptoed down to find Mammy wasn't there and Daddy was asleep in his usual place. She searched everywhere in the house but Mammy just wasn't there and she couldn't dare to wake Daddy up. It would be a long time before any of the others came home from school and Lulu got very scared all alone. Even though Daddy was there, she felt more alone than ever.

She knew that Mammy sometimes used to say she was going to run away with a Kilty! Lulu never knew who they were, except they were like those men who played the bagpipes as they marched in their uniforms dressed in kilts. Because some days, Lulu used to hear the bands playing as they marched down the next road and she would run down to see them, even though she wasn't allowed to do that.

And their Pied Piper music always brought Lulu to tears of excitement and shaking all over.

And marching bands with lots of people still do!

# Fear Sets In

All sorts of scary thoughts filled Lulu up when all she could hear was the noisy empty house, with Daddy snoring in the wee chair. And houses make a lot of sounds when there is nobody else there. Listen sometimes to the silence.

She was so, so full of fear until she believed that Mammy was never coming home again.

Did you ever get that scared when you imagine things that are so big and your mind makes up a whole big story in your imagination and you can't see anything the right way anymore? Lulu knows now that we all do this and we scare ourselves half to death about what might happen that we can't see anything straight anymore or ask for help. Even big people do it, except they can usually cover it up more by pretending to be more important or talking like they have all the answers, or saying nothing.

Lulu knows now that we can just drop straight into our hearts and dream into a time when everything felt right and when we were full of joy and laughter and peace. Looking at the sky for a tiny bit of blue helps or feeling our feet really solid on the earth is great too. Or singing our favourite song out loud is a great one.

Lulu stayed upstairs in the silence until Daddy went back to work and the house was completely empty.

That noisy silence of squeaks and hums and ticks and tocks. And just nothing.

She looked in Mammy's jewellery box and everything was still there. But her coat was gone. She stretched out her attic bedroom window as far as she could even though it was thirty-six stairs up. Lulu always counted the steps up and down. There was no sign of Mammy.

It was a long horrible time waiting for the door to open. Later, Perfect Sister and Play Brother came home from school, but Lulu doesn't remember if they were worried or scared because they seemed to go away and do their own stuff somewhere else.

Back up in her bed, Lulu could tell the time in the evening when all the children in the street had their dinner and were out playing together, and it was strange to hear them, but know she couldn't go out today to join in. And then, it started to get dark and all the children drifted back home until the street was silent.

After what seemed like a long scary forever time later Mammy did come back home. She never said where she had been until years and years later, but Lulu knew she was very sad.

Nothing actually happened that afternoon except that Lulu didn't like it and she didn't understand it. She was just so relieved that her mammy came home again and saved her from all her imaginings of being completely alone. But the fear and dread got stuck inside for a long, long time.

# God Comes

One time when Lulu was sick but was getting better enough to be downstairs in the sitting room at night, watching TV with everyone, she was snuggled up beside Mammy on the settee.

She felt so safe and warm there and fell asleep. Not completely asleep, but in that sort of woozy place where it is too good to wake up and too good to sleep and miss the lovely warm safe feelings.

Mammy knew it was time for Lulu to go to bed, but because she didn't want to wake up, Mammy decided she better carry her up to bed.

And she did. Mammy gathered Lulu up and began carrying her the whole way up the stairs, and Lulu just didn't want that feeling to stop, so she kind of pretended to stay fast asleep all the way up.

It was a long hard climb for Mammy and Lulu has often wondered how Mammy managed to carry her the whole way. And when Lulu was all tucked up warm in bed, she felt bad for making her mammy have to carry her all that way, and really didn't know how she did it at all.

A long, long, long number of years later, Lulu realised when Mammy was carrying her, then God must have been carrying Mammy. Otherwise she never could have managed it. And that feeling still gives Lulu the goose bumps!

# Lulu and Her Granda

Up until Lulu was 3, her beautiful Granda lived with them all in their house pub, the biggest red brick corner building called the Star and Garter. What a fancy name, even though Lulu never knew what it was meant to mean.

Painted by Biggest Sister

Lulu loved her Granda so, so much and was always following him around.

Every afternoon, he would sit on the wee corner wall of the railway bridge across from the house that was right beside the shore.

He would sit and smoke, walking stick in one hand and his pint of Guinness in the other. He had lovely, smelly clothes, all smokey, and woody and thick with age, and a flat cap.

His face always seemed to have a settled smile and his eyes sparkled.

Granda always had time for Lulu, and Play Brother loved him so much too.

Sometimes, he would let Lulu have a sip of the froth of his Guinness until her lips got covered in the bitter yellow foam.

It seemed like every day, Granda, Lulu and sometimes Play Brother would go for a walk together. Under the arch and along the shore to the wee steps, sometimes as far as the big pier and back. Sometimes, though not very often at all, Granda would lead them back through the inside train station arch, where they shouted for their own echoes, then up the slope again to come back home past the houses. And sometimes, but really not very often at all, Granda would find a halfpenny to buy Lulu and sometimes Play Brother a penny chew. Those days were very special.

Granda never seemed to be in a hurry, not like when the big ones would have to take Lulu out with them when they went out to play at the shore. They all hated having to take Lulu with them, probably because she was always tripping and falling, and used to always sing the song that was very popular then called, 'Don't bring Lulu!' It went like this:

*'You can bring Pearl she's a real nice girl, but don't bring Lulu,*
*You can bring Rose with her turned up nose, but don't bring Lulu!'*

Lulu doesn't remember anything Granda ever said on their conversations, which they must have had lots of, because she was always with him. She just remembers the love and kindness and gentleness of her Granda. He always had time.

Remember how Lulu keeps reminding us of how we store all these feelings inside, especially in what we can see or hear, feel, smell or taste?

Well, right now, even though she is very grown up , she can still smell his clothes and his smoke, and she can still taste the frothy Guinness and it fills her full of Granda's love, because that love, that extra special wonderful love, never ever leaves our hearts.

Right now, she smells the smoke and burnt smell of the morning after the station fire when the little sweetshop inside in the corner was burnt out.

Even though it's not a nice smell that we would want around our house or clothes, this smell brings her right back to Granda and his big heart, for it was very big indeed.

That morning when there was still smoke coming out of the station roof, Lulu and Play Brother begged Granda to let them go and see.

Everything was black and grey and chokey smokey.

It was so strange to see all the sweets scattered on the ground, and Granda might not have seen, or pretended not to see them searching through with our hands to find any that seemed still good enough to possibly eat.

And they did find some and went home happy and excited with Granda, and Lulu reckons they probably didn't tell it at home, in case they got into trouble!

Their secret would have been safe with Granda anyway. He probably had lots of his own secrets too if the wrinkles on his face and the twinkles in his eyes were anything to go by.

Lulu loved Granda so much.

Lulu, this grown up woman telling you this still does love him so much, 'cos no one can ever take the love out of our big hearts, even if we forget it's there sometimes.

When Granda died and went to heaven, Lulu's big brothers and sisters have told her many years later that she tried to climb inside Granda's coffin with him, as he laid with the lid open in the big room.

How could anyone believe he was gone, and that she couldn't go along with him? Why did he have to leave her?

Anyway, actually, he is still right here, now, not in a way that Lulu can still sit on his knee, or drink his Guinness or hold his hand on a walk, but inside, with all the smell, taste and warm feelings in her big heart. This is what love is. It never dies, maybe it just changes shape or comes in when we are on the shore watching the tide coming in or going out. Or smelling those smells that sometimes appear out of nowhere, and that's when Granda is here.

Lulu loves you so very much, Granda!

Granda

# Falling

Lulu was always tripping up and falling, and she still has some of the scars on her knees and her face. No wonder the big ones hated having her tagging along, as they always had to pick her up and drag her along to keep up.

She just didn't seem able to stop herself running everywhere and jumping across walls, just for the fun and thrill of it all. Like, running back up from the wee shop with a message for Mammy, and hopping across the wee wall so she didn't touch the path. *Trip! Bang!* Crash headlong into Mrs Murray's windowsill face first! Blood and more blood!

Playing up The Avenue – a 'Strictly Private' lane with a few posh houses tucked away behind all the trees and bushes on each side.

Lulu just loved going there with her two little friends after school. Making houses and brushing the forest floor clean with brooms made from twigs. Or climbing high up a tree when there was any sound of a car coming up the lane. It was important to hide because the owners would come out and shout at them to leave!

One day, Lulu was still wearing her beautiful cream-ribbed tights that Mammy had bought, and they were very expensive ones.

Up the tree, she went as far and as fast as she dared when the fright of a car caused her to fall off the branch. Down she tumbled until her tights got caught by a branch and Lulu carried on, like she was on an elastic rope or a parachute!

The tights ripped all the way up the leg but did a wonderful job of saving Lulu from bad cuts and bruises. Poor Mammy darning these!

The day they were all playing hide and seek was very exciting. Lulu ran as fast as she could up the hill and knew she had to hide quickly, so she rushed headfirst into a narrow passageway. Except it was barred off with barbed wire and Lulu pushed her face straight into it!

She didn't think of crying just yet, as she slowed down and slowly tried to loosen her face off the spike. But it ripped across. More blood and a beautiful scar that still shows sometimes all these years later when Lulu gets embarrassed or confused. All those beautiful scars still telling their story. Except the ones on the inside aren't as easy to see. We all only feel those.

Or falling badly on the ice runway they had made on the night they poured lots of water over their neighbours' back path, because it had a wonderful slope that really did need to be made into a proper ice rink! Lulu never wondered what the poor woman thought of that the next day when she tried to walk out of her gate and down the path.

Or finding ways to get down all the thirty-six stairs without ever touching the floor. Over the top bannister, slide down for nine steps. Climb off over the big wooden post at the end. Stretch across to get onto the eight stairs top. Fall off. Start again. Jump down all five to the lower landing. Fall. Bump head on stair. Then the final fourteen steps by stretching, jumping, sliding.

You get the picture! Just walking down the stairs never entered Lulu's mind! Or falling into the bramble bushes where you sometimes went to have a pee, so no one could see you, and falling in! Nettle stings all over Lulu's bottom!

Or jumping off the shore wall in a competition to see who could jump the furthest, then putting out her arms to save herself. When out jumped a big sharp piece of metal and stabbed Lulu's hand, right in the centre. That scar is still there too!

Or the day Lulu just desperately wanted a bicycle to ride and decided to borrow Contented Brother's racing bike. Contented Brother didn't know of course. Lulu had only just learned how to stay up on two wheels because on one evening, the big ones had held the saddle for her, as she wobbled along on the big bike that was so tall she couldn't get anywhere near the seat.

So Lulu wheeled his bike out of the yard and leaned it against the wall so she could climb up and get her leg over the bar. She had to keep the bike leaning over a bit just to be able to pedal at all down the back alley, dragging the toes of her sandals on the ground most of the way like brakes. She was getting braver and decided to go all the way down Park Drive on the road. But the bike got faster and faster, and Lulu couldn't reach the brakes and didn't want to fall by putting her feet down, so she decided to try and turn at the bottom of the hill, straight down the hill and past the stop sign where the other road crossed and straight into the wall of the parish hall! Bent Lulu, bent bicycle, but thank heavens, no cars driving across as she flew through!

Contented Brother wouldn't have been pleased at all, but Lulu only remembers the thrill of it all! Life was all very exciting and had to be enjoyed at top speed!

Sometimes, not knowing what could go wrong is just perfect, otherwise, how would we ever dare? I dare you!

# The Ghost Alley

When it got dark early on winter evenings, sometimes they got out to play, and sometimes, Lulu could find an old torch to take out with them.

At the bottom of the back entry, there was Mr. McKimm's huge wooden shed, painted green. It was a great set of doors to play two ball against, and it wasn't very often that you could have two balls, but that's another story.

As it was getting dark, a whole group of small kids and bigger still-kids gathered at the bottom of the shed. Next to the shed was a skinny little alleyway that led up past the backyard gates of the houses on the Downshire Road. At the top in the darkest loneliest place, you would hit the wall where you had to turn left along an even darker part to get to the road and the streetlights. Or right into the forbidden pathway past the gardens, and along the big tall stone wall that divided them up from the back entry to our backyards. Beautiful roses grew on that side of the wall.

It was always the dare, a very scary dare to go up the alley on your own, and sometimes without even a torch. Either you could creep up very slowly to be ready for any ghost that might jump out, or run as fast as you could to get through and out the other side. Lulu was always terrified, but excited at the same time.

Do you ever feel like that when you don't know if the excitement in your belly and the tingling all over is better to listen to than the fear that makes your heart pound? It can be hard to tell the difference, can't it?

Anyway, no one could dare to say NO, because that would make you like a baby and then nobody would want to play with you anymore.

Sometimes, one of the others would sneak up the lit Downshire Road and hide around the darkest corner, ready to jump out on you as you turned the scariest bit at the top. Shrieks of laughter and terror filled the air, until they were all together again outside Mr McKimm's shed.

Tales to tell each other another time, even when they are all so much older and when they can admit that sometimes as big people, they still get scared and excited all at once and don't know whether to risk it or run away.

Lulu knows life is full of ghost alleys.
Ghost alleys full of all the shadows of what happened to us, or what we saw or heard, or smelt, or tasted and felt.
Ghost alleys without a torch. And ones that jump out at you.

Back then, they screamed it out and laughed hysterically when it was over, when they felt safe again. The perfect reply. Instead of squishing down those feelings inside until they can't breathe, and pretend. And big important people need to learn to do that again until the light comes back.

Lulu has done both these things all through her life, kept it all in or let it all out. Mostly, Lulu still lets it all out even though that can upset people, especially ones who have spent their whole lives learning to keep everything stuffed inside. But her big heart always leads her still to her next adventure, helping other big people and not so big people to be brave inside, when they look inside their hearts with love, not fear. And learning to be their own light, their own torch inside. And it never matters if we do the thing or if we don't, because the most important bit is to feel, so we can know our heart and follow that.

# Thunder and Lightning

Lulu and the other kids around, especially Peter, couldn't resist playing thunder and lightning. When you knock someone's front door like thunder and then run away like lightning.

How those poor people must have felt in their house in the evening, just settling down for a rest at the TV? They never got any peace.

It's funny how everybody always feels like they have to answer their door when it knocks or the bell rings. Even though they don't want to be disturbed. A bit like when someone's being nasty, big people don't always remember that they can decide to hear it or not.

But Lulu never even thought of that, because it was so exciting and just plain fun to take the chance most times she went past, especially when she was out playing with Peter. Especially Mrs Brown at number ten, because hers was the easiest door to reach and escape from, and Mrs Brown was such a lovely, friendly person. Lulu never seemed to think how annoying it must be to be pranked so often. It wasn't that Lulu didn't like her at all, just the excitement and fun of the dare was too big to let in any sense about how it must have been for Mrs Brown.

Funnily enough at these times, Lulu never even considered that she might tell her Daddy on her, which she can't ever have done, even though it's fairly likely that she always knew who was doing it. Thank heavens Mrs Brown was so loving, because there would have been terrible trouble if Daddy had found out.

But then, the most terrifying and properly scary, was Mamie! She was a very different kettle of fish…whatever that was meant to mean.

Mamie was a little woman who was nearly as wide as she was tall and she was very scary indeed.

She lived on her own and she did not like people at all, especially children.

She always wore a green uniform with trousers, a black belt of leather and a beret on her head that covered her black short hair. Lulu wonders what war she was always ready to fight in!

She never spoke to anyone, except when she was selling water to the bands and followers when they paraded down past her house, or yelled at the children if they came near her front door.

And they all knew for certain that she had an axe!

Peter, Lulu's best and boldest friend, always took dares that nobody else would.

He was brave enough to run up to Mamie's door and run away as fast as he could. Lulu only remembers being brave enough to do this once and it was probably the scariest thing she ever did!

They would run away as fast as they could and hide up the back entry or the ghost alley and wait. Mamie came out to her gate and shouted, "I am going to get you. Just you wait! I know you're there and I know who you are." They would hold their breath and wait a long, long time until Mamie slammed her door and went back inside.

One dark night, when somehow Lulu and Peter were out exploring, away down at the parish hall, Peter decided to knock Mamie's door.

But she was ready for them! Perhaps she had started to sit behind her door all day long just waiting to catch hold of one of them. How very sad is that?

She opened the door and they began to run. She went back inside for a moment but rushed out again, and they really did know then that the stories about the axe were all true!

They ran and ran, down the road, and along the next street, and then somehow, they got split up.

Big people say, 'Every man for himself,' and that is when ships like the Titanic sank, and nobody has time to save anybody else, the captain allowed everyone to just try and save themselves from certain death! Lulu saw that in a film. But this was real!

Even though Mamie was nowhere to be seen now, Lulu ended up racing up the darkest longest alley, which she never ever normally even dreamed of doing and hid in a back gateway. The gate was closed, so she had to lean up tight against the gate like they do in the films, and hope and pray that her wheezy chest wouldn't give her away.

Lulu stayed there for a very, very long time. Everything was so quiet and Lulu almost had to stop breathing so she could hear if Mamie was coming, and not just hear her big heart pounding and booming in her chest.

Finally, Lulu knew she had to go home or they would be sending out another search party for her.

Like a soldier in the war films on TV, Lulu crept up to the top of the alley, always ducking in for shadowy cover, before finally daring to see if the coast was clear, so she could cross the road to get to her street.

Lulu did make it home alive, and of course, never told anyone what happened, or could have happened, and she has no idea where Peter went that night, except that he was very, very scared as well.

And that was the last time ever that Lulu dared to go anywhere near Mamie's house. But Peter did, because he never could resist his big heart and all that excitement.

Nowadays, Lulu wonders if chasing them all the time was what gave Mamie's life all her thrills and excitement. Maybe, just maybe, Mamie wouldn't have had anyone to remind her she was still alive inside.

Grown-ups can get very lonely and don't know how to say so.

# Peter

Lulu's friend. A boy outside and different from all the boys in the family. Being outside, from another world of his own family lets the light shine in from another angle. Peter lived just up the street and together, they had many adventures and always seemed to find each other to play together when they both needed to explore, dare and be more of themselves.

Peter always dared far more than anyone else she knew. He was so important for Lulu simply because of this. With him, Lulu could be more of herself, more free, more everything. Sometimes, his more-ness was too much for Lulu and probably too much for him at times, but they needed each other to help set themselves free, away from adults and bigger ones who seemed to have forgotten how to play.

They sat on the little wall, made and ate fresh mud pies, of sticks, little stones, muck and water from the puddles. They used a big magnifying glass to set paper alight, amazed at the power of the sun.

They dug a great big deep hole in Lulu's next-door neighbour's path so they could find Australia. Though they gave up after a while of digging out great big rocks, and perhaps finally realising that it wasn't good for Mrs Murray's path.

They knocked all the doors and ran.

They dared each other to swallow thorns off the rose bushes, and picked and stripped the rose hips to reveal the itchy seeds that they pushed down others jumpers. They pestered the little woman in the corner shop with, "Vera, how much are your penny chews?" They laughed.

One day, after being up The Avenue, they very boldly crawled into a posh families' back garden and played on their swings until the father came out and chased them, telling them he would get the police.

They brought the little wreck of a bike Lulu had been given from someone else's rubbish, with no chain and flat tyres, to the man everybody knew could fix bikes. Any bike was better than none at all. He was called Dodger, but Peter and Lulu had no idea why he was called that then. Down they went to find his backyard, way down near the chapel. In they went and said, "Hey Dodger, can you fix our bike?"

Well, he chased them. He scared them! He was very cross and didn't seem to like them at all. The cheek of them calling him by the name that gave away exactly what he got up to. Laugh and shake and run, and laugh again.

They scoured the chapel gardens, up close against the wall to the primary school, where you could find balls that had been lost by other kids when out playing at break times. They played in the chapel and Peter would sneak up into the balcony and play the organ. Peter was an amazing musician.

They drank the holy water when they were thirsty and chewed the candle wax, but it was nothing like bubble gum.

But sometimes Lulu just loved to be inside in the silence and the empty space, with God and Mary. When that special gentle love just filled her heart and the whole space.

They robbed orchards and crawled into other people's gardens to pick some of their flowers. They talked and put their little worlds to right.

And so much more, as they grew up into teenagers when everything was changing, and that's the story for another page, another time.

Thank you, Peter. My real friend.

# Robbing Orchards

So, about other people's apples. Usually, they gleam out at you over someone's wall or hedge and always seem too high to reach, and call out, "Pick me! I am the juiciest!" And there was always the really exciting risk of getting caught. And Lulu would watch in total awe at the bigger ones who always seemed to find a way to get over the wall, or find a hole in the hedge to get in and get some apples. And windfalls didn't really count 'cos they were usually bruised or wrinkled and, well, too easy to get.

Mrs Colgan, who lived in the lovely little bungalow across the street, was a very nice old lady living on her own. Even though she was just across the street, Lulu knew nothing about her really. And the only time she ever spoke to her was when the big ones would get Lulu to knock her door and ask her if she had any windfalls picked that she could spare. Dear Mrs Colgan would always talk to her and probably never found out that when this was going on, the big ones had crawled through her hedge at the back and managed to climb the tree to get the most scrumpy little red apples. And Lulu never really knew how important her part in the robbery was. But she loved getting her share of the apples, and especially the pears.

Mr McKimm's garden higher up the street, had two big trees that you could get to, by daring to go down his driveway at the side of his house. You had to be very careful which ones you got, one was sour and one was sweet.

One day, when Lulu was playing with a girl called Hilary from the next road, Hilary told her that Mr McKimm was her uncle and that he was in hospital sick. Somehow, they decided to go and steal some apples, because no one would be there to catch them. So, for once, Lulu and Hilary just walked down the drive, fearless, and got an apple or two when they noticed a huge gooseberry bush. The gooseberry hairs were standing out all shiny from the nearly red fat balls of juice, a bit like how the hairs stand up on your arms when a shiver goes down your spine. And the thorns didn't matter so much because the gooseberries were just perfect for picking.

So, they lifted up their skirts to make like a basket and filled them up with gooseberries and because Mr McKimm was in hospital they decided to sit on his front step, right up against his big blue door, and eat their feast. Delicious! Then, the big door opened all of a sudden and there stood Mr McKimm!

Lulu doesn't remember what he said, only that they jumped up, spilling all of their stash, and fled as fast as their legs would carry them, and away down the street.

Maybe they got away with it because he was Hilary's uncle, or maybe he was still too tired from being in hospital, but Lulu was so relieved when he didn't come to her house to tell on her!

And Lulu didn't really think she was actually stealing, because stealing is very wrong. But you see, there were so many apples and pears, just hanging off people's trees all autumn long, and surely, it couldn't have been a too bad thing to do when they were only going to go to waste anyway, and it was all just so exciting that Lulu's heart couldn't resist. So much fun!

# Lulu's Perfect Sister

Perfect Sister was a whole four years older than Lulu but she always seemed so much more grown-up.

As far as Lulu could tell, Perfect Sister was always perfect and Lulu always knew that she could never be that!

She doesn't think she was ever jealous of Perfect Sister, just in wonder at her and all her lovely things, and how she always seemed to look so neat, clean and tidy.

Lulu was such a nuisance to Perfect Sister and she knows Perfect Sister really hated her, because Lulu always seemed to have to tag along when she went down the shore or even up into the big bedroom, or had to go to Mass with her on Sunday mornings at nine o'clock. But especially because Lulu always managed to get into Perfect Sister's things.

Everything of Perfect Sister's was always perfect, beautiful and special, and Lulu really did her best to copy her, but she just couldn't seem to be like that, and things would just break in Lulu's hand or get messed up somehow.

Perfect Sister had a great idea one day that they could make themselves little dressing tables, since the only drawers or tables in the big attic room belonged to and were strictly the private property of the bigger sisters. And all five of them shared the attic room.

She took Lulu to the greengrocer's and they got used empty orange boxes that were made out of thin white wood that weren't too heavy to lift, and had a middle piece sort of shelf that looked just like a bookcase when stood on their ends.

Perfect Sister was always very clever too, so she made them some little curtains out of old pillowcases that they pinned up on old string across the front. She might have let Lulu help out but probably only on bits Lulu couldn't mess up.

Anyway, as if by magic, they each had their own private little dressing table where you could set pretty things on top and pull the curtain out or in to keep all the lovely things safe inside.

Perfect Sister had such beautiful things that never seemed to break.

On Saturdays, when they got sixpence pay, Perfect Sister carefully selected and bought another beautiful little bangle. These were proudly displayed at the corner shop and every one had little chips of beautiful coloured shiny plastic glass on the outside so they sparkled as you moved your arm. Before long, it seemed like Perfect Sister had about ten or twenty of these that she loved to wear. Lulu tried to copy her, as usual, and bought one or two but they always broke so she stopped doing that.

She had a special secret box of wood with some sort of shiny pearly stuff set into the top. This box was never to be touched nor opened by anyone and that mostly meant Lulu. But Lulu really wanted to explore the special box and try on all the gorgeous rings, bangles and things, and so when off sick from school, she searched everywhere to try and find the box but it always seemed to be moved from the last place Perfect Sister had hidden it, and Perfect Sister always seemed to know when Lulu had been in it. And Lulu knew it was not right, but she just couldn't help herself. Curiosity always seemed to get the better of Lulu.

There was a beautiful set of coloured pencils inside the box and Lulu did manage to find those one day. She just couldn't resist drawing with them all, but of course, the leads got broken and Lulu probably chewed the ends of one or two, though she doesn't remember doing that.

Perfect Sister really hated her for this, and Lulu understands why, now.

It was like there was never anywhere in Lulu's big family for anyone to find space to just be with themselves surrounded by only their own few chosen beautiful things.

There was nowhere to hide away from everyone and everything, and there was no one to help make sure anyone else didn't take your things, or understand really.

It was like everyone had to try to learn their own way of being themselves, without any help. Or find some space inside themselves when there was no space outside with so many others, who all had the same need and longing.

Except our biggest sisters, who were so grown up and very glamorous, did seem to privately understand all this. When they started going to work, they would sometimes buy Perfect Sister and Lulu special presents.
Lulu knows they were saying, "Don't worry, we understand and we want you to feel safe and loved and special."

Lulu still wonders who did that for them when they were trying to grow up, because there really wasn't anyone there who had the time or the space to make them feel specially loved! And she knows some of the terrible things they had to go through or get through when they were the ones who got picked on or put down! Or how they had to go after school to bottle the Guinness and get it all labelled and ready, or look after Lulu. Or pretend not to exist.

This still makes Lulu sad.

Biggest Sister and Mammy Sister brought them home toys or little handbags from Donegal, and bangles, and baskets for Easter. One time, Biggest Sister sewed a special fur bunny rabbit each for Lulu and Perfect Sister. Biggest Sister must have known how Perfect Sister looked after everything and Lulu didn't, or couldn't, because Perfect Sister's was pure white with pink ears and beautiful pink glass eyes. And Lulu's was brown, just brown, with brown eyes and fur that was rough.

Perfect Sister kept her bunny in an old Easter egg box with a clear plastic top and ribbon where her bunny fitted perfectly, and kept it on top of her dressing table.

And of course, that's another thing Lulu couldn't resist playing with when Perfect Sister wasn't there, because it was so soft, beautiful and white.

# The Blue Anorak

The worst time for Perfect Sister and when she hated Lulu the most, even though it wasn't Lulu's fault, was over her precious new anorak!

The grammar school uniform was very important and Perfect Sister got a beautiful school blazer, as well as her gaberdine overcoat, when she started there, although Lulu still doesn't know how Mammy was able to afford all that. And Perfect Sister's uniform always looked so clean, neat and tidy and, well…just perfect.

One day, Biggest Sister came home with a new anorak for Perfect Sister. It's important to remember anoraks had just been invented and hers was navy blue with a diamond pattern stitched in and a long zip and a hood. And it was so beautiful and all the rage.

But on that day, and Lulu remembers it very well because they were in the kitchen, and Perfect Sister tried on her wonderful beautiful new anorak. But Mammy made Lulu try it on and zip it up over her chest, and Mammy announced that the anorak had to be Lulu's, because Perfect Sister already had that very expensive school blazer, as well as a gabardine coat. And so, it was.

Even then, Lulu knew just how completely and totally wrong this was, and that Mammy should never had made that decision. And Lulu knew from the first moment how angry, sad and frustrated Perfect Sister was, and she never felt good when she wore Perfect Sister's beautiful coat. And Perfect Sister hated Lulu for even existing then, and Lulu understands why!

Sometimes parents can seem really cruel, and really don't seem to understand at all what it is like to be a child, never mind a child who is trying to learn how to grow up. And sometimes, parents need to just listen and notice, even though they may be busy and struggling through all the washing, shopping, cooking and ironing, and all of their own feelings.

And Lulu knows that sometimes, children need to scream, and fight, or shout and cry and get angry, so they can make enough space inside themselves again to be able to get on with the tough business of being young.

Like the time Separate Sister, who had started work and was always very, very gorgeous looking, started to cry in the kitchen. She wailed. She sobbed and shrieked, and cried, and cried, and sobbed and sobbed. And she couldn't stop, not for hours, and Mammy didn't know what to do or how to help. Mammy even tried slapping her face, like you see in the old movies, but that just made her cry and cry all the more. Lulu and Perfect Sister were afraid as they watched when they were supposed to be doing their homework, because they just didn't understand and didn't know what to do. Lulu remembers Separate Sister's eyes all huge, red and swollen after hours and hours of crying. And she seemed so far away, buried inside herself, too far away to be reached.

Lulu knows and always knew in a way that sometimes, we have to do these things to just clean up our big hearts so they can shine again. It's our job to look after our big beautiful hearts! And maybe, thank heavens, Separate Sister did cry so much then, or goodness knows what would have happened if her heart had stayed so full up with tears.

And maybe if Mammy had been able to do those things just for HERself, or had someone to make her feel loved and loved and loved, then she would have found a different way to get Lulu a coat.

So, for years, Perfect Sister hated Lulu. Of course, she did. Lulu completely gets it. But Lulu and Perfect Sister were really lucky many, many years later to say all these things to each other, to become real sisters and friends and to love each other forever more.

Much, much later, when Lulu was all grown up and finding out so much about herself and about Perfect Sister, she realised that she was never meant to be the same as Perfect Sister. What a very silly idea altogether. I mean just how can anybody be the same as anybody else, except if you're twins, and even then, just because you might look the same, every one of us has our own heart, our own spark of the light.

It really would have been very helpful if Lulu had known then that it was okay just to be yourself! To feel. And she wishes Perfect Sister had known that too.

Lulu now knows that Perfect Sister needed to be perfect, and she was very, very good at it. It was what Perfect Sister needed to do so she could feel safe, and have a way to try and control everything that did happen or might happen or could have happened, or could be imagined into happening. And Perfect Sister was so good at it that people saw her as special and beautiful, and so did Lulu, and she was.

Even though it's very, very sad, Lulu needs to tell you that Perfect Sister died and went to heaven far, far too young. She had got married and had a beautiful little boy, but still she was very, very young and too young to have to die!

One day very soon after she died, Lulu and Separate Sister were sorting out all Perfect Sister's drawers in her beautiful perfect bedroom. Every last little thing had been perfectly sorted, folded and laid out. Deep inside in one of the drawers, Lulu found all those shiny pearly little bangles that she had bought when they were very, very little, still perfect and neatly tidied away in a drawer. Lulu cried the deepest cry and laughed and remembered how perfect Perfect Sister was, like right now just remembering this. And you know what, she always will be! Perfect!

Lulu, on the other hand, was never built to be like that, and couldn't be even if she tried. In fact, the more Lulu tried to be anything other than herself, things usually went wrong. Like walking down the street in her new shoes, trying hard to look pretty, confident, and sure, when bang, up comes the pavement and trips her so she fell straight onto the ground right in the middle of the road! Or always looking scruffy and with a mucky collar on her white school shirt and her hair all wrong, so that the nuns would take her aside and tell her she was nothing like her sister. Perfect Sister, who was always perfect, and always looked nice in her uniform.

Or the awful day when Lulu proudly wore her new indoor shoes for the first time, and Mother Paul stopped her and told her she would have to go home and couldn't come back until her shoes were right! Lulu never knew her shoes were slightly wrong, and she cried and cried and was made to feel stupid, and well, all wrong.

And so, Lulu somehow started to believe then, but only dimly, and not in a way that she knew it was happening deep inside, her big secret, that she just wasn't good enough.

But that one time, thank heavens, her biggest brother stepped in and wrote a letter for Mammy to sign, that said these shoes would have to do, and the nuns shouldn't have made Lulu cry like that.

Oldest Brother's big heart was well and truly open wide for Lulu that day, even though he was too big for her to really know anything about him, and she loved him for it.

Mostly, Lulu just did what she did, and loved everything as much as it was possible to, and didn't even think about what could go wrong. Those feelings and foggy grey clouds inside only started to notice much later.

People have a habit of saying 'look before you leap' but for Lulu, it was always the other way around. Leap and then maybe, if you have to, look!

It has always been that way for Lulu, and probably always will be, and sometimes, that works perfectly. Other times, Lulu has to think about and do everything she can to fill the love up again in her big heart, to make her feel okay again when things have gone wrong.

Do you ever have to do that?

# Separate Sister

Beautiful Separate Sister didn't just cry. But she was definitely separate. Maybe because she got sort of looked past, being right in the middle of the family, or maybe because that was her way of keeping hold of her own big heart. She used to wander away a lot too. Perhaps we all did.

On those special days, when everyone sang their song, their solo, she always sang 'Nobody's child'.

*'I'm nobody's child, I'm nobody's child.*
*Just like a flower, I'm growing wild.*
*No Mammy's kisses and no Daddy's smile,*
*Nobody wants me. I'm nobody's child.'*

But nobody really heard what she was saying, what she most needed someone, anyone to hear. Sometimes we really have to listen, because one way or another people always show us what they need.

Lulu remembers her as being very daring and very grown up. She always let boys come to pick her up from the door at home, and that seemed a very brave thing to do. And she always dressed in the most beautiful very, very, very short dresses. She used to iron her beautiful hair at the ironing board which always seemed very odd to Lulu.

But Lulu really didn't know her then at all. Somehow she was just like a stranger. That makes Lulu sad now.

And Lulu suspects Separate Sister only really let herself become herself when she was away from home. And in fact, that this was probably true for every one of us. So probably, none of us really knew each other or ourselves when we were growing up together, because we all had to squash ourselves up very small and tight so we could disappear and be safe inside ourselves. Inside OUT and Outside IN.

# Mammy Sister

Mammy Sister was always very, very good at being everything a mammy is. She had to practise this a lot when she was very little herself, because she always had to look after Lulu when Lulu was very tiny. Mammy had to work behind the bar as well as everything else, so someone had to take care of Lulu, and she can still feel the little Tansad pushchair that Mammy Sister pushed her around in, along the shore. Hard and bumpy but safe.

Mammy Sister still tells Lulu about the day, away along the shore, when Lulu choked on a sweet and poor sister had to do everything she could to get her to breathe again. But the thing Mammy Sister remembers most is how two women who knew them just stayed sitting on the wall, watching and did nothing to help her save ME!
A little girl, carrying such a responsibility, all alone, and nobody helped.

In the girls' attic room that all five of them shared there were three beds, and Mammy Sister had to share with me. She never even complained when Lulu wet the bed! How loving is that!
Mammy Sister saw a lot and felt a lot, and had to be very grown up way earlier than any little girl should have to be. She was the first to leave home when she got married very young, to her very own handsome prince, to live happily ever after.
She had a very special party before her wedding day when all her friends came round and the big table was set in front of the sitting room window with all her beautiful wedding presents set on top. Perfect Sister and Lulu were so excited to see lots of other big grown up girls come round, and laughed and giggled on the stairs listening to all the chitter chatter. And wondering if they would ever find a handsome prince.

It seems like all the girls in Lulu's big family had to leave – escape - as soon as they could, to become themselves. And for some long years, all the sisters had to leave each other behind too. And for a long time Lulu was the only sister left.

# Biggest Sister's Heart

Biggest sister was always beautiful. Like a perfectly dressed elegant lady, and somehow, separate too.

The story Mammy always told was that she was only supposed to live until she was seven because she had a hole in her heart!

Lulu couldn't even begin to understand what that meant or how that could be. It must be a terrible thing to have been told that. Just how does anyone go on living a long happy life when they are not even supposed to be alive anymore? Too upsetting and confusing.

Lulu was very little when Biggest Sister had to go in for a big operation to close up the hole. Only many years later did Lulu come to know how hard that was on Biggest Sister.

But then Lulu really wanted to do something very special for her when she was coming home from the hospital. So Lulu spent hours and hours making a big welcome home poster and had it all ready hanging over her bed. She was sure that this would be lovely for Biggest Sister to see and know how much she was loved. Lulu got all her brightest colouring pens and painted a great big red heart, and then in the middle, she made a great big black hole with an arrow through it. Lulu was very pleased with her work!

Well, it all backfired. Of course, it did!

How could Biggest Sister like to see that? She was very, very upset and hurt and tore it down. Then, Lulu didn't understand what she had done so wrong.

All Lulu had wanted to do was to show her how happy she was to have her home again, and how much she loved Biggest Sister. Still does.

It seems that all of us can only show love in the way that we can understand what it means. And sometimes, the way we show it just doesn't manage to reach the other person. Maybe that's because we can't see what love would look like and feel like to the other person. So, what are we meant to do with that?

Perhaps, Biggest Sister wanted to be made to feel safe again, and to be looked after and told what a miracle she is, and treated to beautiful things, and cared for, in whatever way that felt right to her.

What way do you like to be loved? What sort of love wraps you up in its safe soft blanket and lets you know everything will be okay? And maybe it would help if you let people know that so the ones who love you know what to do.

# Sundays Were Special Days

Sundays were special days in the house and different to all the others because the pub wasn't open and so Daddy and the big ones would be at home all day. Everything in the house was different when Daddy came home, and everyone had to put away their fun, noise, normal fighting and messing about, and be something different, a very quiet different.

Some Sundays were special because of the bad things that happened when everyone was at home together, and had to behave to keep Daddy happy, and others were special because of the lovely things that happened. Thing is you could never tell which way it would go, and everything could change very, very fast, and so it seemed to be better to always be on guard.

Lulu mostly loved when Daddy would take them all on long, long, long walks away along the shore, past the second shore field, past Clanbrassil and the river, past the yacht club and away along past the golf links that came right down to the beach.

He would help them hunt through the long grass to find the golf balls lost by the not-so-good golfers. They were real treasures, because later, Lulu could pick off all the hard white outside, deeper and deeper, until she found the hard rubber bouncy ball at the centre. This was great fun! Though mostly, the older boys got to keep the golf balls for serious things, like golf. And of course, they shouted at Lulu, again.

In autumn, Lulu loved it when the apple trees were hanging with big apples that were always much too high for Lulu ever to reach. They were always it seemed, best and juiciest when they were growing in someone's private garden.

One Sunday, Lulu remembers Daddy holding her up high above his shoulders behind the great stone wall, so she could pick and eat a wonderful red apple.

So, really, it was Daddy who taught Lulu to rob people's orchards. And so, to this very day, other people's apples always light up with Daddy's love and closeness for Lulu. That is how memories work!

Sometimes, they would walk away up the hills and it was a long, long walk, up the Church Road past the Nut Glen and along a long windy little road with grass growing up the middle and then back down the Whinney Hill and home. Just walking and walking altogether, picking blackberries and feeding the horses and of course, stealing apples. Lulu was always happiest when they were outside in the countryside or on the shore. And she still is.

On the best Sundays, the happiest ones, nobody got shouted at or hit at the Sunday dinner table. And the big sisters didn't have a go at them when they had all that washing up to do. Twelve people make a lot of dirty plates and pots on Sunday dinnertimes. And Sundays were the only day where all of them ate together for dinner and tea, with two big tables set out and perfectly laid and huge apple tarts made by Biggest Sister, Mammy Sister and Separate Sister on Saturday evening. Lulu watched in amazement as they made and rolled the pastry and created the golden sugary treats for Sunday tea.

When the older sisters had escaped to their own lives, Perfect Sister and Lulu took over the girls' jobs of cooking, cleaning and shopping. On Sundays it was important to get everything right.

Perfect Sister always knew that she and Lulu had to be back to get the big Sunday tea ready for everyone, on the dot of seven o' clock. She made sure she was there to get everything right, but Lulu was up the hills, talking to the horses and feeding them straw, or along her forever beloved shore. And Lulu only just managed to get back on time to help set everything out ready.

Sunday mornings meant Perfect Sister and Lulu had to get up for early Mass so that they could be home when the big ones all went to ten o'clock Mass, and they had to have their breakfast cooked and ready the minute they walked in the door. Some days, Perfect Sister would faint in Mass, and that was scary. Lulu didn't know what to do to help when that happened. It was probably because she hadn't had any food, because you weren't allowed to eat until after communion on Sundays, and Perfect Sister was growing up a bit, and things were changing in her.

Some rules make no sense at all! If you are going to get sick and faint, then surely it's sensible to make sure you eat something, no matter who says you shouldn't. And surely, God wouldn't mind. Lulu is sure that God wouldn't ever want anyone to get sick.

Sometimes, it's really hard to figure out what rules are right for your heart and what ones are just like somebody else's hand-me-down dresses that are too tight round your neck, or too big and you feel all wrong inside when you have to wear them. But Lulu wants you to check inside when feelings choke you like this, because for sure, right in that moment, you can choose if you will listen to your heart or not! And the more time you spend inside your heart getting to know all the love that is in there, the easier it gets to know.

# Making Breakfast

Making Sunday breakfast was always such a nerve-wracking time.

They had to make sure the special bacon was perfectly cooked with no burnt bits and then as Daddy sat down, they had to fry him perfectly soft eggs. That's hard enough for grown-ups and chefs to get perfect every time, and somehow, there was always something wrong for Daddy. In fact, there was always something wrong with some one of them all the time. And it was very hard to get everything right so it wasn't going to be you that got it!

You see, they all knew someone would get picked on. Lulu is sure they all knew, even though some of them have decided to forget things like this.

Daddy was a waiter in hotels when he was very young and had to leave home to look after himself, and he was very good at it. But somehow, he expected them, the girls that is, to serve Sunday dinner like they were in a fancy restaurant. Lulu never ever managed how to hold two big spoons together in one hand to serve the vegetables. And twelve hot dinner plates were very big and heavy to carry and set down to everyone at their right-hand side, and very often Perfect Sister seemed to get the blame for getting things even a little bit wrong. And of course, the more we get all nervous inside, the more we make mistakes, don't we?

Like that Sunday, when the hot gravy boat slipped off the plates and went all down the wall, or the Sunday when Daddy ripped the little rings Perfect Sister was wearing off her fingers. Lulu still doesn't understand why, but she knows it was not right for Daddy to be so cruel. Perfect Sister felt angry and sad for her whole life because of times like that. Lulu knows this because many, many years later, Perfect Sister was able to tell her. Why did he have to pick on her all the time?

And Lulu doesn't know how Far Away Brother feels inside nowadays, except maybe even further away, because of how he was always made to eat with his knife and fork the right way wrong way round, when Daddy was there, because he was left-handed, and that wasn't allowed!

Lulu is absolutely sure that God would have something to say about that stupid rule too!

# Telling It

Lulu expects that some of the bigger ones won't like Lulu telling all these things out loud now, because it will make them uncomfortable. She also knows that they have lots of memories like this too, because some of them have told her. And of course, the biggest ones didn't have anyone they could copy and often ended up having to be so big and grown-up so they could help Mammy look after all the young ones, or for the boys to find a way or a place to practise being men. And their beautiful hearts must have been so confused, sad and scared a lot of the time too.

And of course, telling all this, Lulu always understood the one big rule in their house even though nobody ever said it -

'You never let anyone outside the family know what really goes on inside the family, inside the house'.

So outside, like on Sundays, when they all went to Mass with polished shoes and shiny faces, everyone would tell Daddy how wonderful and important he was, and how he had raised the most perfect big family. He seemed so happy and pleased and proud. But inside…?

Families are very confusing.

And which place do we end up pretending the most, or do we end up doing it everywhere? At home or outside? Lulu's never been any good at that, and she's glad!

Anyway, now, Lulu really understands that she has to follow her heart. Not to make anyone feel bad, but to let all the love and light in for all of us. Like opening all the windows, and doors to let the wind blow right through. A lot like drying the sheets on the line to make them all bright from the sun, and smell beautiful again.

# Sunday Drives

Some of those Sundays, Daddy would decide to take Mammy out for a 'wee run' in the car. That meant the car was crowded out, but mostly, it was Perfect Sister, Play Brother and Lulu.

They very often ended up at Portaferry along narrow little roads over the hills and by the shore, and Daddy used to always make them jump and sometimes feel sick and laugh when the car seemed to fly over the bumps in the road.

Mammy and Daddy would go into the little hotel for a drink, and they got to play on the pier and watch the strange big car ferry that took lots of people and cars over to Strangford. Lulu could never understand how the boat didn't sink because the water was very rough and choppy, and they opened the back of it so cars could drive on and off.

Some days, Daddy would come back out and give them a shilling to buy ice creams or sweets up in the little corner shop on the hill. These were indeed good days, but sometimes, he didn't give them money. Lulu still doesn't understand why not and it was confusing and disappointing too. Mainly because it was impossible not to imagine and dream of all the lovely ice cream and sweets that could be bought. They were always told by Mammy never to ask him—not for anything.

One very special day, Daddy drove them all the way to Carnlough, just Lulu with Mammy and Daddy, and Lulu looked longingly at the little shops with all the buckets, spades and beach balls hanging up outside. One big ball, as big as her arms could have held, captured Lulu's heart. It had all the colours of the rainbow splashed all over it, and Lulu imagined it could bounce really high. But she didn't dare ask. They kept on driving and probably stopped somewhere further on for a drink.

Lulu did happen to say how beautiful it was and how much she loved those beautiful colours of the sea, the sky and the sun. This was instead of just asking, because she knew not to do that, so she just mentioned it, secretly wishing and hoping that it was hers.

On the drive back past that shop, Daddy saw the huge big ice cream statue outside and stopped so they could all have one.

Somehow deep inside, he must have heard how much Lulu wanted, needed that ball, and somehow, somehow, he gave her a whole half crown, to buy it. A whole half-crown! Daddy could be really kind, and Lulu was so glad in her big heart to know that. That ball was very special to Lulu and always has been, all through her grown up, important life.

Sometimes, she still takes it out with her to play in the street, (in her mind's eye that is), and she can feel all that joy and love very brightly indeed. This is very useful even now when Lulu wants to feel better inside herself and bring the rainbows into her heart again.

# Sunday Evenings

On Sunday evenings, after they came back from the chapel again, the fire would be lit in the sitting room. Lulu loved when they would go in there in the dark and play blind man's bluff together, while Mammy and Daddy were in the kitchen. They had to be very quiet, of course, but in the dark, someone had to catch them as they all crawled and crept behind the sofa, the big armchairs, or behind the curtains and get ready to jump out or get away before they were caught. Lulu loved that scary excitement when they all played together like this.

Sometimes, play fighting would start but mostly someone ended up in tears. It always started as Play Brother would ask if Lulu wanted 'funsies' or 'realsies'. Lulu always just wanted it to be funsies, because she knew she couldn't win a real fight with her big brother. But somewhere along the way, he would change it to realsies without asking, and Lulu never could win, and it hurt.

Sometimes people change the rules and all of a sudden we don't know how to play anymore.

But Lulu knows it was all fun and games and all part of brothers and sisters finding ways to play together, and to find out about themselves and how strong they could be. And it always seemed like boys had to be able to show how strong, brave and manlike they could be, and a good way to test this out was probably on wee sisters!

Lulu sometimes wonders then, what boys are supposed to do when they feel frightened or upset. It doesn't seem fair that they always have to pretend to be like big men! And it must have been very difficult with our Daddy, because he was always being big and strong, and he was the boss. So how were they supposed to be like that? There could only ever be one Boss!

Later on Sunday evenings, Daddy always laid out the table in the kitchen to count all the money from the pub from the week. It was very serious and important work. Lulu would watch how he counted out all the notes and carefully set them in piles, and then all the different coins in stacks. Then, he wrote it all down in his little book and put the money away safely in the safe. Maybe that's why it was called the safe.

Lulu, Perfect Sister and Play Brother, all secretly hoped he would leave some out for them to have as pocket money. Some weeks he did, and some weeks, he didn't, but of course, they never asked. He never ever gave the money to them, but set it on the mantelpiece for them to find later. It would have been lovely if he had given it to them, into their hands. What makes it so?

Lulu never ever understood why he only left it for them sometimes, except that maybe he liked to play tricks on them so they would never expect anything. And Lulu also knows that was a very sad thing about her Daddy too.

Even now, all these years later Lulu finds it really hard to just ask for what she needs or wants, without hiding it or dressing it all up in hints. The funny thing is it usually came true that she didn't get what she needed, almost as if she had planned it that way so she could keep believing that it's not okay to ask.

Imagine how much easier it would be if we all just asked for what we need, and finally scrape out those beliefs that seem to get buried inside without us even knowing it! Imagine that!

After the money was all counted, on some very special Sunday evenings, Daddy would lay the big purple cloth on the table and get the dominoes out and call them in to play. Sometimes, he would let them have loose pennies and half pennies as their playing money.

Lulu just loved those games, even though she was so much smaller than all the others and never really understood how to play properly. But once in a while, somehow, Lulu did manage to win and she still doesn't know if that was because the others let her, or she was lucky. All those brown smelly coins for buying toffee and lollies! It was just so lovely when everyone was so happy as they all played together with Daddy. Remembering these nights still makes Lulu feel all warm and fuzzy inside.

On some Sunday nights, Daddy would have his friends around to play cards together and have some whisky. They took over the big table in the kitchen that got covered by the big purple cloth. The only thing was, nobody could get to the scullery for a drink or for something to eat, because you had to go through the kitchen and past all the men, two times, in and out again.

Lulu used to stand at the kitchen door, sometimes with Perfect Sister and Play Brother and listen to try and work out the best time to dare to go in. Those big men frightened Lulu, because they were so big, especially the one they all called Big Mick, and they always wanted to pick Lulu up and Lulu did not like that at all. Sometimes, they would rub their big horrible spikey beards against Lulu's face and laugh. But Lulu didn't laugh. She hated it.

Sometimes, she was told to sing for them all and had to stand up on a kitchen chair singing Hail Glorious St. Patrick or another hymn. This never seemed to happen to the others, but Lulu was usually given some money when she finished singing and then, she could escape again. Even so it really was not nice, not nice at all.

Big Mick once gave Lulu a very special silver necklace with a beautiful picture of Our Lady carved into it, though it lay without a chain, all black and dull in a box for many, many years. Lulu remembers. She was only about five and he gave it to her when he was leaving the house one day and they were standing on the front path together.

All these years later, Lulu has polished Mary up all beautiful and shiny, solid silver. Lulu still has that beautiful shiny big round medal made of silver and still wonders why he gave it to her. As she is writing this, she has been wearing it every day.

Because it is full of Our Lady's love, perfect love that lay waiting to be seen and felt and cherished. And she changes colour and reflects her blue light to remind Lulu she is always always present.

Sometimes on Sunday nights, the whole big family would all sit together in the sitting room with the TV on and the big fire lit. Lulu and Play Brother used to always sit on the floor because there weren't enough seats for them all, but that was okay.

Oldest Brother, whom she didn't really know at all, had started working in the pub and had money now of his own. On some of these evenings, he would send Lulu and Play Brother down to the picture house sweetshop to get his sweets. Always half a pound of Riley's chocolate rolls, yummy, and some other kind too. There were so many chocolates in those paper bags. Chocolates that little ones could never afford to buy. They even cost more than a lovely new rubber ball! A new ball with that yummy new smell that only on very, very rare days Mammy would buy from that wee shop. Lulu and Play Brother always stole one or two sweets when they were walking back up the street to home. Of course, they did!

Oldest Brother always wanted to keep his sweets just for himself and not share them, and Lulu understands this now, because it was very difficult to keep anything just for yourself in this big family.

One of these nights, they had all been asking him for a share, and he kept saying no, so Daddy snatched the bags laughing and threw them all up in the air. They scattered all over the room and everyone laughed as they scurried around grabbing what they could.

Everyone laughed except Oldest Brother, who of course couldn't have said anything, and Lulu understands now how upset he would have been, because he had earned all that money to buy them himself, and he deserved to have nice things just for himself, like a kind of reward.

Everybody needs to give themselves that love! A reward!

At special times, Mammy got lots of great big, enormous chocolate boxes, with pretty pictures and ribbons on from customers from the pub. Some of the boxes were so big, Lulu couldn't stretch her arms to carry them. And it was really special when Mammy would open them and let them have a share. Oh that yummy smell in the box, and that beautiful big ribbon. But all the best ones were gone before Lulu got her turn to pick.

A bit like the big tin of biscuits that got opened after Sunday dinner. Lulu always wanted to taste the pink wafer ones. There were two in every tin. Of course, she never really got to have those because, as she was the baby of the family, she got to pick last. Usually, only the plain ones left or custard creams.

One day, when Lulu became a big grown-up, she was teaching people about loving the little child inside themselves, her favourite subject, and she caught herself doing everything she could to get the pink wafers at break times. One day, she pushed one into her mouth and realised she didn't even like the taste which was like some horrible perfume. It tasted disgusting! Lulu laughed and laughed when she realised how sometimes we do things we don't actually like even when we are grown-ups, because we are still trying to get that feeling back from when we were little.

She loved little Lulu more that day and knew more about how big people have big hearts too, even if they do things that they actually don't like, because the little them inside pops up when they least expect it.

# Money

Money seemed to be a very important thing in their house. Daddy always seemed to have lots, and Mammy always seemed to have not much at all. And sometimes Mammy would shake Daddy's trousers upside down when she was tidying them and gather up all the loose change and notes that fell out. Clever mammy.

But if Mammy hadn't taught them not to, and they had asked Daddy for things, then Lulu would have got the bicycle she always wanted, or the beautiful hard Irish dancing shoes that Mammy couldn't afford, and meant that Lulu had to stop going to Irish dancing lessons, or learned to play piano, instead of just listening with a glass through the wall to the piano teacher woman with her pupils.

And if they had asked Daddy for things, then maybe Daddy would have learnt how to be kinder, and he would have been happier because all his children and Mammy would have been happier too. Then, he might have been able to feel loved!

Lulu always wanted Daddy to be happy. It felt like one of the biggest things she wanted and had to do, and Lulu knows Mammy always wanted Daddy to be happy and kind, and like the handsome young man she first fell in love with, because she told Lulu stories about how she fell in love with him way back then.

But she must have been afraid a lot instead, because he got cross so much. And so, Mammy probably felt she had to try to keep the peace, and taught them to be quiet when Daddy was home, to never do anything that might upset him, and never ask him for anything - like she didn't. And so, that's what they all did, in their different ways. But that meant that sometimes, most times, Lulu and her big brothers and sisters forgot how to just be themselves, like children need to be.

It's as if each one locked themselves up inside, to be safe somehow. But the thing is, it's easy to lose the key.

Have you lost your key?

# Asking

Now, Lulu can see how she carried this all the way through most of her life. Never ask for anything you need or dearly want. Hold the secret longing inside and don't show how you feel.

 Then of course, what most big people don't realise is that this need leaks out the more we try to hide it. Like a big picture house board with big lights, it displays the very thing we are trying to hide for everyone to see, or hear or pick up somehow.

It seems to Lulu that the more we get all tight inside, then somehow, we send out invisible signals that other people can't actually see, but they can feel. Like our heart is reaching out and one way or another, touching everybody else's and then that kind of finds the same part of the other person's heart. Like it finds the bit of them that feels tight, angry or whatever, and if they don't like feeling that bit, they get grumpy or horrible, so they don't have to feel it inside themselves.

And if we are kind of softer and have let our hearts be open, then people pick that up as well, and don't feel the same need to be cruel.

This happens all the time. It's just that big people, who look important, and sensible, and who seem to be right about everything, are very good at hiding their hearts, even from themselves, in case anyone sees.

Little people are better at letting their hearts show. It's only later when the whole world seems to want us to be sensible, and not to laugh or cry in the wrong places, like Lulu did.

But I mean, what are you supposed to do when all these big feelings rush up and really want to come out? Swallow them down like a big lump of dry bread? Or stop breathing and make your chest wheezy? Or find a way to pretend?

Lulu didn't know how to do those cover up things for a very, very long time and when she did end up doing that years and years later, she got sick in another way. But that's to tell you another time.

And now Lulu is very good at seeing other people's big film screen all across their heart, and it shows up in how they walk and how they talk and the way their faces tell the story. And right now, Lulu just fills up with love for all her family, and all those people, and their own special film in which they are the star! And she wants all their movies to have a happy ending or a happy beginning starting from right now!

Just ASK!

# About Daddy

Lulu loved her big tall strong Daddy very, very much, (until she started to have to grow up and raged against all the fear and silence and power and everything else). and it is really important that you know this now. She does again now!

She didn't love him in a warm cuddly kind of way. More like she was in awe of him and scared of him too and she spent a lot of time watching, listening and wondering how she could find a way to get him to see her and how much she loved him, so that he could show even a little bit of love back. And she was so very confused because everyone in their house was afraid of him, even Mammy.

So Lulu really didn't know how to be or what to do, probably like all the others.

One Christmas, Lulu had gathered all her money and bought little presents for Daddy and Mammy and wrapped them all beautifully. She even bought special Christmas Sellotape with Santas on that was very special. On Christmas morning, Lulu was very, very excited to give Daddy his present, to really let him see how much she loved him. He was sitting in his wee chair at the fire reading the huge newspaper. Lulu came in quietly, figuring out the best place to sit beside him…not too close…not too far away. She waited and waited for him to stop reading a moment, but he didn't.

Finally, she stretched out her arm holding the precious gift and said,

"Happy Christmas Daddy!"

Silence. Not a flickering, as if she hadn't spoken or he hadn't heard. Big breath, "Happy Christmas Daddy, here's your Christmas present." Heart racing. Chest tightening.

Nothing.

Not a sign that he had even knew she was there, but he must have because she was very close and did speak out loud and surely, he couldn't have missed the big box pointed at him.

Nothing.

In the end, Lulu just had to set the box with all its love, down on the chair beside him, and walk away. How could he do that? What did she do wrong? What could she have said instead?

How could Christmas have been made all wrong all of a sudden?

Why would Daddy do this?

Lulu, in all the messed up, confused feelings inside her must have decided to stay back after that. And she had to try and work out all by herself what that was all for, and what she would try to do about this big jumble of feelings. So she just buried them deep in her heart and carried them around like a big cut that won't heal, for years and years and years.

What Lulu couldn't possibly have known then, because she was so small, is that it wasn't her job to make her Daddy happy, and in fact, it's not even possible that someone else can take all the responsibility for making anyone else feel happy inside themselves.

THIS IS VERY, VERY IMPORTANT TO KNOW!!!

Imagine, if everyone in your family, or in school or wherever, knew and agreed that it was all of our jobs to find our happiness inside and to be just that and nothing more. Lulu believes that would solve a lot of problems...when everyone's hearts could just shine, and then people wouldn't get so sad or hurt or crinkled up inside.

Years and years and years later, Lulu knew and understood, that Daddy never had any kindness when he was just a wee boy, and that life was very difficult for him, and sometimes, he didn't even have shoes to walk to school. So he just didn't know how to show his big heart, because he had lost it somewhere when it got buried deep inside him. And maybe that explains how he needed so much whisky so he didn't need to feel all of that sadness inside him.

And even though Lulu has just told you this, she really, really didn't know that it wasn't her job to make Daddy happy and keep him happy, and that it's impossible anyway.

What was she meant to do with all the love inside then? Lulu could really have done with someone, anyone to help her work all that out. But then, Mammy didn't seem to know this either. And nobody ever talked about things like this.

I love you, Daddy!

Now, this grown-up grey-haired woman, has once again experienced how this old wound had never properly healed. Somehow, as Lulu comes to life here on these pages, all the biggest patches and scars that hadn't been properly healed, have come back, the old memory relived in different clothes now.

This memory of the offered gift of love rejected or withheld, stepped right in again today, with such force that little Lulu inside felt the knock more powerfully than ever since that day.

The memory hadn't been healed and hung around until a smell, a sound, an experience burst through in life's drama.

This time, however, the grown-up Lulu has taken the time and felt the pain fully, like Lulu could not bear to. From the tears and sadness, into the light and love. Love from the grown-up Lulu to that little girl with the promise never to stop listening to herself and always to be delighted to receive Lulu's gift of pure love. The memory has been healed.

Yours can be too. Love yourself enough to reach out from the pain.

# And Mammy

Lulu's lovely gentle, sad, quiet, tired mammy! Mammy who was always there, singing in the kitchen, loud shouty singing of 'How Great Thou Art' while she banged the pots because she was upset, or soft love songs because she remembered being young and carefree. Mammy who had to get the broken window or chair fixed after the boys had a fight, and make sure it was all done before Daddy came home for his dinner.

Lulu loved how safe it felt being with Mammy, but she didn't know how much Mammy needed love too, not for a long, long time. And Lulu didn't imagine until lots of years later, how things could have been so different if Mammy hadn't been afraid, and had let herself say out loud to Daddy and to herself what she thought was right, what she wanted to happen and how she felt. And asked for love. Or decided that her way of being a loving mammy was right, or taught him how to let love lead the way.

Mammy, who had all this dark blood coming out of her, terrifying black and flooding, no matter what Mammy tried to do to catch it. Lulu saw it one day when she went into Mammy's bedroom and saw her. And all Lulu could understand, was that it was something to do with having had all them babies, and how she nearly died when she had Lulu, and how the doctors told her she couldn't have any more or she would die. Even how the priest had to come to give her something called the last rites when she was giving birth.

Lulu didn't know what to make of any of that, except Mammy was sick and it had something to do with her being born, and that Mammy could die. So, Lulu became very, very afraid of hospitals, because Mammy had to go there to get better, and the nuns in black costumes walked around very quietly when they went to see her on Sundays. They scared Lulu. And Lulu was afraid Mammy wouldn't come home again.

But Lulu also knows that her Mammy knew that she was always loved by her own daddy, that was Lulu's Granda. And that was how she was able to sing a lot and be so kind and gentle, even when she was having to do all the washing and cooking, and making sure Daddy didn't get upset. And how she always managed to find a penny to buy a chew or a lolly, or let them have a lemonade bottle that really belonged to the pub, to get the penny back on it.

And this might be how Mammy would listen to the hundreds of questions Lulu seemed to ask every day, and always sing this song as the answer…

*'Que Sarah Sarah, whatever will be will be,*
*The future's not ours to see Que Sarah Sarah!'*

Lulu always wondered who Sarah was, and why did Mammy always answer this way.

All Lulu could understand of this song, was that her Mammy didn't know the answers and that it was a very sad song for Mammy. When she sang this to Lulu, it's as if she went away back to some other place inside her. A place that she had lost and longed to go back to. And then, she would sigh.


I love you, Mammy. Thank you.

# For All You Mammies and Daddies

Lulu knows this. So, listen please!

Every Mammy and Daddy in the world love their children, don't they? I mean, they must do because together with God, they created us. And they can only love their children from what they know, from the way they knew love when they were little and from their experiences as they grew up and found their way in the world. Well, that is until they decide to find out about their own memories and all their ghost alleys and happy times. Then, they can love themselves, first, before trying to work out how to love their own babies.

And it's easy to blame. But blame just covers our hearts up and is of no help. And as little Lulu has shown you here, little children pick up everything…all the little and enormous things they see, hear, taste, smell and feel. And it doesn't even have to be what happened to them, but also, what they saw happen to other people. Or it might even just be a story they heard.

And somewhere in the middle of all the business of growing, every one of us starts to use all those feelings whenever we have to figure out how to be. We use them like we watch movies or play old records, without even knowing it.

Somewhere along the line, we can lose that little beautiful free loving heart that is just who we really are. Covered up with other people's clothes and smells and rules. Memories that want to speak.

But Lulu is here inside me and your pure loving heart is inside you longing to be free. And we can change the movie, because we are all the actors and the director. Imagine that!

Everything is LOVE! Or everything is a longing for LOVE! Or fear. And Lulu loves love!

# Easter

New shoes for summer, pretty dresses, hats and socks, even if some of these were hand-me-downs from bigger sisters, and an Easter basket!

Easter eggs were very special and Lulu's Biggest Sisters used to work in Joe's chocolate factory when they were growing up, so they were able to get Easter baskets with chocolate and little yellow fluffy chicks and a ribbon on for Perfect Sister and Lulu, and Play Brother would get a boy's egg.

They were all stacked up in the big glass bookcase out of reach until Easter Sunday arrived. Anyway, the big bookcase was too high to reach up and dangerous because of all the broken glass edges at the bottom, where the boys had accidentally hit the glass when playing marbles. One year, there was great trouble because someone had got at all the eggs, including the extra ones that been hidden in the wardrobe.

Every single one had been opened, partly eaten and then wrapped up again. The funny thing is that no one ever owned up to doing it, and even to this day, it makes Lulu laugh because to this day, she doesn't know who ate them. But Lulu also knew no one would have dared admit it and Lulu understands that.

On some Easter Sundays, the whole family would go on a day trip to Donegal to Daddy's homeplace. Lulu still can't work out how everyone fitted into the car, but she does remember how Perfect Sister, Play Brother and her used to sit in the boot looking backwards out the window. There was so much fun and laughter as they made faces at the people in the other cars to try and get them to laugh too. Lulu always laughed a lot.

It was a long, long journey to Donegal, and when they got there, they would go to visit some of Daddy's brothers and sisters.

For Lulu, it was like landing on a different planet or something out of a story book and she was amazed at how different everyone was and spoke. They all seemed so strange.

The tiny stone cottage that Daddy grew up in with his fifteen, yes, fifteen, brothers and sisters, was so small.

They would arrive up the little lane and see the white walls and the red wooden door that was split in two. Lulu knows now that that was called a stable door, so you could open up only the top half if you wanted.

There was only one room downstairs with a big turf fireplace at one end and a wooden table under the tiny window. It was very dark inside, except for the light from the fire or the top stable door.

The floor was made of big stone slabs and Aunty Mary always made like she was surprised to see them all, but she had the little table with its oilcloth cover set and ready with China cups and plates.

She always put a big load of homemade fruit bread on the table, with cake and tea. Maybe that's why her hands were so big—to make bread and milk the cows.

They all talked so strangely too and Lulu used to stand in wonder at the whole place and wonder where her children all went to bed at night or where they went to the toilet even! She now knows that there were one or two rooms upstairs and somehow, everyone managed to squeeze in to sleep. But imagine when there were fifteen children when Daddy was growing up in there! And the stone walls and the flagstone floor held all the memories of all the lives that were born, grew, lived and died here.

Shoes and legs and new white Easter bobby socks always got mucky visiting here too because of the chickens that ran around outside the door and pooped everywhere, and also because of the cow pats up behind the house where they used to go through the long grass to find the well.

One Easter, they arrived to see the baby's cot outside the door in the sun. Yes, the baby was asleep inside, but surrounded by lots and lots of little baby banty chicks. These were the real baby chickens that they tried to copy for Easter baskets but so warm, soft and real, and Lulu got to hold one in her hands just for a minute. The little chicks were kept in there to keep them safe but also and mostly, to keep the baby warm. Imagine how your own big fluffy feather duvet nowadays is, and that the little live chicks probably did a better, but probably funnier job of it.

Then, off to fancy dinner in a big hotel. All of us in a big long line at the table with white linen tablecloths and so many knives and forks each, and napkins and waitresses in black uniforms with white frilly aprons. It was all a bit scary. Trying to be on best of best behaviour and not spill anything or do anything wrong. And then having to eat everything on the plate, the soup, the dinner and the dessert. And poor Perfect Sister, who hated the soup, and wanted to be sick but couldn't let Daddy see her avoiding it. He always made her swallow the foods that made her feel sick, especially fish.

Not a nice time at all.

After a while, they all loaded into the car again and down to Bundoran to see Aunty Bridie. Aunty Bridie had a shop at the front of her house and here, she sold all sorts of useful things, but all Lulu could see were the jars of sweets and the chocolate bars. It was very exciting to have a few pennies to be able to buy a big bag of Lulu's favourite chocolate toffees. Of course, needless to say, Lulu then got sick when they were driving back up the long road home.

These were very special Sundays where Lulu got to see inside a totally different storybook world to the one she lived in, but she wouldn't have wanted to stay there forever. Because home was home.

One of the big, big cousins called Mark was always very odd, it seemed to Lulu. When he sometimes came to visit and sometimes decided to stay over, he would always eat all the spuds and biscuits, never ever thinking anyone else might like some too.

Once, he came in his brown tweed jacket, and the strange thing was there was a big brown leather button sewed on to the front of the middle of the arm. Not anywhere where a button could be useful to button things and nowhere near any buttonholes or anything else.

They couldn't resist asking him why the button was there at all.

Lulu still laughs today at his very sensible but very silly explanation that a hole had appeared on the arm of his best jacket and he sewed the button on there to hide the hole!

He always seemed to be a very strange man indeed.

On Easter Mondays, Mammy would take them all for a picnic which was very special indeed. And very free. It was very rare to get a whole day with Mammy just having fun.

They would take sandwiches and the eggs they had boiled hard and painted, with Whin bush flowers to dye them bright yellow, for rolling down the hills above the nut glen. They would walk and walk and Lulu just loved being out having fun with Mammy and all the others.

On this one Easter Monday, somehow, Lulu got her shoes and socks all covered with sticky rabbit poo, and it was all up her legs and, on her knickers and dress. Mammy wasn't very happy about this, and when they got home, she made Perfect Sister take them up to the bath to wash our feet and legs. Not a whole bath, because there wouldn't have been enough hot water, but one thing led to another and somehow, Lulu fell in and got all her clothes wet and mucky and Perfect Sister got the blame again. Sure, of course, this was Lulu.

But they laughed and laughed about it for a lot of years. And Mammy wasn't really cross, not really.

# The Shore

Lulu always escaped to the shore, since she was very, very little, and even before they moved out of the pub house when she was only three. The shore was just under the railway bridge outside their door.

In fact, it was the place everyone seemed to go and spend as much time as they could there, away from everything grown-up, and serious and busy. It was freedom!

Along past the wee steps, and on to the Big Pier where lots of children would go and jump in off the end when it was warm enough to go in the water.

There were sailing dinghies that they called yachts at the big yacht club there, that was always marked 'Private', 'Members only', and very posh, though that never stopped Lulu from going in to explore anyway.

There were two fishermen there who had big boats with motors that they took out in the evenings to go fishing and always seemed to take quite a few others with them. But usually, this was only the older boys, and Lulu doesn't remember any girls going out with them.

One of the fishermen was called Joe Salmon! What a perfect name that probably explains how he ended up being a fisherman, though he usually caught mackerel or herrings. With his beautiful bright blue wooden boat that always seemed to need painting, and a lovely engine that gave out a yummy oily smell and made lovely gurgling sputtering sounds when he headed off from the Big Pier to go fishing.

Lulu always so wanted and wished that she could go out fishing in his boat, and used to sit at the deep end of the pier and always ask, "Mister Salmon, can you please take me out in your boat tonight?"

He always pretended not to hear her and she wondered how come all the other, mostly boys got taken on board, down the rickety steps and onto the boat that seemed to bounce and bob about as they climbed on board. Lulu always stayed waiting until they came back, and could see way off in the distance, out where the big ferries used to sail, when his little boat would appear again on its return journey with loads of fish. Oh to see and smell the mackerel with their blue, and silver, and green and gold shiny skins, and she loved them even better when they had some at home fried in the pan, with the skin all crispy.

Lulu really never noticed how late it was becoming or that it would soon be dark, and they used to send out search parties to find her and make her come home.

One night when Perfect Sister was sent to get her home, Lulu wouldn't do what Perfect Sister needed her to do. Lulu just ran into the boatyard and tried to walk along the top of the round metal bars, like a tightrope walker in the circus would, and how Perfect Sister and the others managed to do the whole way along. But Lulu was a lot smaller and clumsier. As Perfect Sister tried to drag her off, Lulu slipped and fell and cut both her knees, again, and Perfect Sister shouted and shouted at her.

But the woman across the street was standing at her front door and shouted at Perfect Sister for hurting Lulu, even though Lulu knows it wasn't her fault. Perfect Sister got very angry back at the woman, and called her nasty names, and the woman, who wasn't very nice at all, said she was going to tell their Daddy.

So, Lulu knew then that she had to go back home with her, because she really didn't want anyone getting into trouble. And going home was always full of fear…you just never knew what would happen, or who would get blamed and into trouble.

Lulu was always in awe of how Perfect Sister could be so strong and clear somehow when she was away from the house. Not like when she was at home. Mmmm.

# The Big Pier

Anyway, the big pier was indeed very big to Lulu. It was a really brave and scary thing to dare to walk out to the end, with its rickety squeaky floorboards that had gaps in, where you could see the tide underneath, a long way down. And the only rail was made of thin hard metal rope and it moved and wobbled as you grabbed hold of it.

Out at the deep end, there was a crosspiece that led to the side steps, but the scariest were the ones like a ladder right off the end down to the sea, and when the tide was full, it was very deep indeed.

Lulu always wished she was brave enough to jump off like lots of the other bigger children did, but she couldn't swim yet, and thought she would drown trying to get back into shore.

But at least, Lulu found the courage to go out to the end, where she would sit and let her legs dangle over the side, and sit and dream, and laugh and imagine. And Lulu came here to this very spot all through her childhood and the very awkward years of learning to be a grown-up.

Lulu isn't sure anymore if she dreamed this or if it really did happen, but that doesn't matter because the dream is as fantastic as anything could be for real anyway. Dreams always are. And so, it is good to dream big dreams!

In this real dream, Lulu remembers just once, when Joe Salmon did take her out fishing in his blue boat, and Play Brother was there too.

It was scary as the boat seemed to wobble about, as if it would topple over, and especially when they got far away from shore, and the big pier became very little indeed.

Lots of them were crammed in together and they chugged way, way out to the end of the lough, a very long way indeed. And it became very, very cold as the wind blew all around them and they got splashed, as the boat bashed through the waves that got bigger and rougher, as they got deeper and further away from safe, dry land. It was very scary.

She watched the bigger ones catching fish by just dropping a string with bread on it down over the side and caught two or three or four all at once when they pulled the string back up.

It was all so exciting, and scary and, cold and wet, but Lulu felt very brave and happy that she had managed to survive the whole thing.

So that's why they always had to send the bigger ones out to find her, because it probably wasn't safe at all for a little girl to be out on her own, late in the evening, and especially because she could have fallen off the pier or got drowned when out in Mr Salmon's boat. And then what would they all have done?

It was always so special to be down beside the pier on the little sandy shell beach when the tide was nearly full but still coming in.

Just digging the sand with some old bit of wood that had floated in, or just her hands, to build a great big fort wall, in a circle, to sit and wait for a wave off the boats, or the tide to come in and surround her. Of course, the sea would always manage to breakthrough and over the sand walls and usually, before Lulu could get out and up the slippery battery wall. And of course, Lulu would get wet, sometimes right up to her knickers that she had tucked her dress inside, to try to keep dry. Joy.

# Visitors to the Shore

Sometimes, hundreds of families would come down from Belfast on the train when the weather was sunny, and these children really didn't know anything about the sea or how big a wash the big ferries would send in. Lulu couldn't imagine what it would be like to not live beside the sea.

But Lulu knew all about the washes, because she learned it from the big ones, and always knew to watch for the ships, and when to expect the wash. There were always two washes off the ships then, a front and a back one, and the biggest wave was always the first one. It was always very, very exciting to look out for the big dark line that would appear very far out across the whole sea, and try to carefully follow it so they could be ready to run up the wall if it looked like being too big.

But the families from Belfast knew nothing about this, and Lulu couldn't imagine what it must be like to live inside a big town where you couldn't get to the sea every day. That would really make you feel all squashed inside.

One day at the wee steps with Mammy, they watched as one family had their rugs and shoes and socks and clothes and towels all set out neatly on the sand, and they went in for a swim.

Mammy and all of them tried to tell them to move everything back off the beach, but they didn't seem to listen, probably because they were so excited to be going swimming, and suddenly, the huge wave crashed in and swept up all their precious things into the sea.

But saying "I told you so" never ever helps anyone feel better.

Lulu doesn't remember what they did after that, but they must have got their clothes back somehow, or they would have had to go home on the train, in their swimming costume, very cold and silly indeed.

Sometimes, other people can see what we can't because we haven't lived it yet. And it can be very hard to get people to listen to that, because it isn't theirs yet. Sometimes, we have to get wet and lose our shoes and socks before we know. And that's okay too.

# The Canberra

One day, when Lulu was three – it was in 1960, the biggest ship ever to leave the shipyard in Belfast, except the Titanic, was launched on its maiden voyage. That's a very grand name for the first time a ship would sail, and the Canberra was very grand indeed.

Lulu was standing very close to Biggest Sister, her oldest sister, who was always afraid of the sea, and all of the ten of them were lined up at the wall to watch it come down the lough, far out in the shipping lanes.

This was the most beautiful huge white ship, all shiny and brand new, that any of them had ever seen, and there were big crowds all along the shore wall.

But some one of the brothers or sisters said there could be a tidal wave from it. Lulu had never known what one of those was until then, but they told her it is when a huge wave grew bigger and bigger way out to sea, and by the time it reaches the shore, it just keeps on coming bigger and bigger and could wash away all of the wall, the houses, the street and the people. This terrified Lulu, as all the imaginings took root, and after that day, she always made sure to watch the grey wash line off every boat, and try to see if it was an ordinary wash, or a tidal wave that would wash her away. And the trouble was, you could never tell until it was too late or nearly too late, because the big wave would only rise up when it came in very close to shore.

Sometimes you just can't tell if something is going to be bad or not.

On some other day, when Lulu was a bit bigger, she and some friends were on the sand building their sand fort walls when Lulu noticed a thin dark grey line out to sea, across the whole water, and Lulu hadn't seen any ship that had gone down, so she wasn't expecting a wash.

She decided she better tell her friends that it was a tidal wave and explained to them what she had been told.

And so the fear started to grow.

The more they watched, the darker the line became, and the thicker too. And the grey thick line showed no signs of other waves. But soon, they all became terrified and got their shoes and socks and escaped before they would surely be drowned and never heard of again.

Well, there was no tidal wave that day, except in all of Lulu's imaginings. And when her friends' imaginings joined in with her, they created a terrible terrifying story, that was absolutely true inside their heads and especially their hearts.

Lulu knows now how we need to be careful of the ideas we allow to build up inside of us, when there really is only an idea or a thought that somebody told us. When this happens, our hearts can get very wobbly indeed, so it's a good idea to ask somebody or tell them how we feel, so they can help us know what is real or not.

And it's really important if you are the one that listens, then you must never laugh or tell children like Lulu how stupid they are. Or even grownups for that matter! And Lulu thinks it would be better if bigger people didn't tell little ones what they are afraid of, or what could happen, because little ones like Lulu believe everything big people tell them, and get filled up with fear that isn't really theirs.

All these years later, Lulu still watches the tide every day, and watches for how high the waves will come up the shore. She played lots of these wonderful games with her own children, where they drew lines on the sand to see who has got the best guess of the big waves coming in. And of course, she doesn't frighten them, but does show them how it's a good idea to notice the sea and the shore when they play there.

Today, many years on, there are now big signs pinned to the fence at the beach that say:

'Beware of unexpected waves'

Now isn't that the silliest of signs? But just notice. Just notice how everything feels and how we feel! Notice for the huge unexpected waves of feelings that come up from nowhere and could wash all over us. And remember our hearts.

# Collecting Crabs

Even without a bucket and spade, Lulu loved to find crabs underneath the big rocks that you could only get to when the tide was out. She probably learned the best ways to do it with Play Brother.

And it was always possible to find an old rusty tin or a piece of plastic on the beach that they could collect their catch into.

The best, biggest and scariest crabs were always under the very big heavy rocks covered with seaweed and mussels, and it took all your strength to pull up the edge to get a good enough look. The crabs here were always grey, green or black though, and not like the lovely giant red ones for sale at the market. And they always knew they couldn't eat them.

Sometimes, Lulu hung a string with an open mussel shell with its orange belly showing, over the side of the big pier when the tide was nearly out and big crabs would catch hold of the bait. And sometimes, though not often, she managed to draw the string slowly up and up until the crab could be set down on the planks. There was a special way to lift them up and hold them that Play Brother showed her, so when you grabbed them by the side edges, you didn't have to get nipped.

It was always a very mucky business and Lulu doesn't know, and didn't care, how Mammy ever managed to get their socks, shoes and clothes clean again every day. Mammy was amazing.

One day, Lulu really was very naughty, and knew she was being such, but it was so much fun and so exciting, she couldn't resist.

It was one day when she was collecting crabs with two of her wee friends, who never seemed to know how to play and have lots of fun properly, so Lulu was always suggesting things and leading them to explore all the wonders of the shore that she knew so well.

Anyway, they, or just Lulu, decided to take the crabs up to the library! Now, the lady in the library was always grumpy and shouted at any children if they laughed, giggled or talked out loud. Lulu didn't like her at all but she did love the library.

So, they went in down the narrow aisles of books, and when no one was looking, they lifted a crab or two and put them behind the books and they were still alive. They didn't actually stay around to find out what happened but Lulu got scared later on because she felt sure the woman behind the desk would guess it was her. Lulu loved to imagine how much she would have screamed when a crab crawled out of the shelf.

Then, they noticed the big red post box outside and looked at the times the postman would come to collect the letters, so they dropped a couple of big crabs into the letter slot. And then, they waited just inside the library front door to see what happened next.

The postman did come and slowly opened the big door to scoop all the letters into his sack. They laughed and laughed. But the funny thing is, Lulu doesn't remember if the postman saw the crabs or if he just ended up pulling them into the sack without noticing. Lulu liked to imagine he got a big shock, jumped and screamed!

Endings can always be anyway we want them to be! Even years and years later, we can decide the ending we wanted back then, because it's all inside us. Isn't it wonderful to know that?

The last stop with the crabs was to the Miss Elliott's sweetshop. The two Miss Elliotts actually lived at the bottom of Lulu's avenue, and their shop in the town was a tiny, tiny little space with two counters joined together. All the sweets and chocolates were displayed on the tops and they sold fireworks at Halloween too. Like the penny bangers or the Jumping Jinnies that Contented brother set off on Lulu when he locked her in the garage, and it jumped after her banging loudly, scaring her half to death.

But the Miss Elliotts weren't very happy or friendly people. Mammy used to say it was because they were frustrated that they never got married, but Lulu knew nothing about all that. Lulu did know they didn't like children, and you couldn't see or feel their hearts at all, probably because they had forgotten they had one, and they probably never really knew any children either. It's so odd to Lulu that they would have a sweetshop mostly for children when they really didn't like them coming in and always stood very stiff and suspicious, waiting the long, long time it took children to choose how to spend their precious pennies.

So, it was especially exciting and daring when they decided, or probably Lulu decided, to put a big crab on top of the sweet counter when Miss Elliott turned away to count the pennies in the till.

Lulu flew out of the wee shop as fast as she could go, with her heart racing so fast and wondering then if they would scream or maybe have a heart attack.

Lulu once again doesn't know what actually happened after that, but she knows they didn't have a fit, and were still there every day, all day long. She never found out if they knew it was her who did it, but was very relieved as the days went by, that they didn't come up to our house and tell Daddy.

What an exciting day that was, even though Lulu knows it was not really a right thing to do. Or maybe it was just perfect.

# Stuck in the Mud!

On another day at the big pier and the yacht club, Lulu went with Perfect Sister and their friend Josie who lived up the avenue from them. Josie was the only girl in her little family, and she always wore the most beautiful dresses, socks and shoes, and she had the most beautiful long golden hair always tied up with a big beautiful ribbon. Lulu always felt that she never really knew Josie at all, because her world seemed to be so completely different to theirs. Josie wasn't used to messing about at the water. That was for sure.

On this one day, Perfect Sister was leading, like she usually did because she was so much bigger. The tide was far out and you could see all the yachts stuck sideways in the mud way far out beyond the big pier, waiting for the tide to come back in so they would float again.

Perfect Sister decided they should take our shoes and socks off, and stuff their dresses in their knickers, then paddle out over the mud to see the yachts up close.

So, they headed out. The mud was very squishy between the toes and came up to their ankles like a gooey grey swamp.

But Josie was a lot heavier than them and she kept sinking into the mud. At one point, Lulu got very scared because she thought of all those cowboy films where cowboys sink into quicksand and never come out again. And Josie sank nearly to her knees, even though sometimes, they were able to pull her out and carry on. As Josie sank, these long red ugly worms with lots of big spines sticking out their sides, squiggled out of the mud all around Josie's legs. She, of course, was crying, and screaming, and they were frightened, or at least, Lulu and Josie were. And that was sensible because they were a long way out from the shore.

But they did reach the yachts and Perfect Sister climbed up into one and they followed her. It was very strange standing on top of the yacht toppled on its side and sitting in the mud. Stranded. Like maybe they would be.

They didn't do anything wrong and just sat there, singing songs and comforting Josie, and pretending everything was okay. But then, this big voice came across the mud booming out of the yacht club loudspeaker that they used when there were races on.

"What are you children doing there? Get out of that boat immediately or I will call the police!"

Oh no! What could we do? We couldn't run that was for sure, because of the mud! Perfect Sister was very cheeky and answered her back, never thinking she could be heard. But, they soon discovered that voices carry a long, long way over wide open spaces, like an echo does, and the loudspeaker boomed again. "How dare you speak to me like that! I am calling the police!"

Well…Josie and Lulu were crying but Perfect Sister wasn't because she was the leader, and leaders always have to be the brave ones. So they all climbed out and dragged Josie as best they could back over the mud to the shore, doing their best to ignore the horrible worms. They did manage to escape and ran all the way home, very, very relieved to see no sign of police. They were very lucky, in lots of ways.

Lulu can only imagine what a shock Josie's mammy got when she arrived home covered in mud from head to foot, and her hair and dress all dirty and messy. Lulu thinks Josie didn't come to the shore with her and Perfect Sister anymore after that day. That's a shame.

Lulu really admired Perfect Sister for how brave, cheeky and funny she was when she was outside home, and could be herself. It seemed to Lulu that Perfect Sister was so squished up inside when she was at home, what with all that effort to be perfect, and having to carry around a very heavy heart, that she needed to be cheeky and bold, and speak back to adults when she was outside. It was like that was the only time when Perfect Sister could practise being as big and tall and equal to big important people who were not very nice.

So, for Lulu, the shore still is and will always be where freedom lives. Where the sea, the tide and the beach change every day without any interference. Where some days, the sea rises up to show its power and washes away things made by people. And where some days, it is so calm and still and clear. And where no matter what we can get back to the centre of our hearts.

Lulu was so lucky to grow up at the shore. She can't imagine what she would have done if she hadn't. Maybe, she wouldn't be here to tell you all these today. Really.

Now you might think Lulu was a very bold rascal when she was little, and you might want to blame her or tell her off! But if you look closely you might be able to see that this was only when she was out of the house and away where no one could make her feel she couldn't breathe, and afraid inside, where someone was always going to 'get it', even if they'd done nothing wrong.

Now, all grown up, Lulu's really glad that her way was to risk it outside being daring and having fun. Not that she planned it that way, it was just who she was. And she wouldn't have wanted to – or couldn't be like some of the others who seemed to decide to always be extra careful and perfectly behaved. Maybe they didn't ever get the chance to just be completely themselves and forgot about the little carefree child inside them. But it's never too late.

# First Holy Communion

Lulu does remember the day of her first Holy Communion though. Her special day! She was all dressed up in the beautiful kind of white dress that had also been worn by Separate Sister on her communion day.

When Lulu came home from Mass, with a lot of her brothers and sisters, Mammy had bought a big box of big cream buns. Buns are always special when they come in a white cardboard box tied up with string.

Everyone was gathered round the table, for Lulu's special communion party. But as soon as the buns came out, the bigger ones all dived in and picked the ones they liked. The only one left was a gooey yellow custard thing with sugar on top. Lulu was so upset, and angry, and, jealous and mad at the same time. She complained but everyone just laughed, so she took the bun out into the street to cry, and threw the bun down the big drain on the street!

It felt so good to do that, even though it meant she got no bun at all, even though it was her special day, and she never ever told anyone what she had done!

Some days, the only thing we can do when no one wants to listen and we feel all trodden on inside, is leave and feel our purest anger. Throwing the big nasty bun of rage and hurt down a drain or a big rock into the sea can be the best answer. And even scream, until there isn't any more to come out. That's usually when the tears come to wash it all clean. Then, we can start to settle again because the feelings have had some space to come up and out of our hearts. And nobody else has to get hurt.

# Dirty Old Men

Now that is a very strange thing to tell your children, especially girls who are too small to know what it's meant to mean, and if they are dirty, why couldn't they get washed somewhere and go home somewhere and not have to want to talk to little girls when they are down the shore playing.

All Lulu knew then, was that she was meant to be scared of dirty old men and to always watch out for one, and get away as fast as she could if there was one anywhere near. But there was no way to know which was which and Lulu seemed to decide to just watch out and be afraid of any man who might be walking out on his own, or sitting on the shore wall or up in the park.

And she was always on the lookout, even on the best days at the shore, or up in the big Ballymenoch Park.

The thing is, you had no way of knowing which ones were the dirty old men and which weren't, so Lulu learned very quickly to be afraid of any man at all. All she knew is that they could do bad things to little girls, even though Lulu never knew what and nobody ever told her, not even her big sisters told her, and they must have known.

Mammy used to tell Lulu, that if a man comes up and offers you sweets, you must never ever put your hand into his pocket to get them, and you must never ever go for a ride in anyone's car.

There was only one day when a man came out of nowhere. Lulu was happily playing two-ball against Mr McKimms big shed and he said he had sweets and asked Lulu if she would like some. Well, Lulu never stayed long enough to find out if he was one of those, or if he really did just want to give her some sweets because he was kind. She ran home as fast as she could and told Mammy all about him. Mammy came down to Park Drive to see if he was there, but he had disappeared.

Ever since that day, Lulu always got scared when any man she didn't know appeared along the shore, or when she was walking up home and some man seemed to be following her every step. It didn't help when she could hear her big sisters talk about the dirty old men that had followed them all the way up from the bus or from the Main Street.

Lulu and her little friends used to love walking away along the shore, all the way to Seapark playground and even as far as the second shore field. Sometimes, Lulu even went that far on her own.

Like the day when there seemed to be nobody else around at all, and it started to rain really hard, and there was massive thunder and lightning. That day, Lulu absolutely believed she might die, and ran as fast as she could to get home and be safe.

She had always been told never to shelter under a tree because it would probably get struck down by the lightning, and you could die.

But there was so many adventures to be had there in the playground, with fantastic rides on the Bangor boats or the witches' hat.

Except for Sundays, when some silly rule people made up about how God wanted all the swings and gates to be locked up because it had to be a day of rest. Blaming God… again!

One day, when the three friends went far, far along the shore, Lulu knew they should turn back, because something just didn't feel safe. The other two decided they would walk even further, but Lulu was afraid and just knew she shouldn't go that far away that day. Something inside just kept telling her to turn back. One of those days when the little voice inside seems to just know what's right and what's not.

So Lulu decided to go home alone and leave the girls to go ahead. Lulu got home safely, but she found out later that day, because their Mammy told Lulu's Mammy, that her friends had been offered a lift home in a dirty old man's car, and because it was raining, they decided to get in.

Now Lulu never ever found out what happened to them that day, because no one ever talked about it. But Lulu knew it was not very nice. Lulu was so glad she had listened to that voice inside her heart that day when it told her to go home.

# When It's Real

There was one day in Belfast when Biggest Sister had taken Lulu and Perfect Sister up to town. It was a very busy Saturday when everybody seemed to be out shopping all at once. Perfect Sister seemed to be starting to grow up then, because she always wanted to make sure she looked nice, and she had just started grammar school. And she was more different somehow.

They were crossing a very wide busy street at the traffic lights beside the city hall and everyone was rushing across before the lights changed again. When Perfect Sister got to the other side, she was crying and shaking because some strange man had whispered something horrible and scary into her ear as he got up close to her in the crowd. Lulu remembers his face to this very day.

Perfect Sister was crying so much that Biggest Sister took them home on the bus as soon as possible and told Daddy what had happened. Daddy did listen that day and took Perfect Sister and Biggest Sister to tell the police, and Perfect Sister had to give a description of the man. Of course, they would never be able to catch him and send him to prison because the street was so busy, and he was gone as soon as they got across.

Lulu remembers he had a horrible smile. She sometimes even now catches herself spotting men who look very like he did, even though he would be dead and gone by now.

Lulu is so glad that Daddy knew how to listen that day.

But there was something else Lulu just couldn't make sense of and she had to keep it a secret inside for a very, very long time.

It was the night when Lulu got up and accidentally saw Daddy having a wee, and she saw this thing between his legs and she was really, really shocked. And she was also very, very scared that Daddy would discover she had seen him.

There was no one Lulu could possibly tell about what she saw, or to help her understand. It was like a secret that everybody knew but nobody talked about. And somehow, Lulu felt embarrassed and maybe even ashamed for the very first time. But she just couldn't understand any of that. Lulu just knew then that men really were very different to women, and knowing this made the fear of men even bigger inside little Lulu.

# Whom to Listen To

Sometimes, it's very hard to figure out whether to listen to the voices inside and to know if they are coming from our heart or from our imagination. And sometimes, it's hard to know the difference between all the scary things bigger people have told us, and whether to listen to that. Or if the excitement is going to lead us to do things that are good for us or not good for us.

Lulu knew it was very, very hard sometimes to find someone who you could talk about all these things to, so you could figure it all out. Like how to figure out which men are dirty old men and which ones are kind and lovely, but she knew it had nothing to do with whether their clothes were dirty or clean.

It seems to Lulu that it would be good if big people would just let little people talk or ask questions, without always leaping in to tell them what they think is right and wrong, or black and white. Or just notice. It is so important to just listen and find out everything that is trying to work itself out inside little ones, so they can learn how to tell what's really going on in their hearts and in their heads!

Grown-ups like parents and teachers seem to have forgotten that, probably because no one ever listened to them properly, and so they forgot how to listen to themselves, until their hearts got all heavy and cloudy. And it's so sad they don't even know that they have that little child still inside themselves, still waiting to be seen and listened to.

# And What About the Boys?

Does anyone help them know when it's okay and right to feel afraid or to feel loving? Who helped my big brothers to love their big hearts, instead of always fighting or messing about? Who helps them now they are all grown up?

Grown up, Lulu really hopes they had someone to listen to them and allow them to speak and clear the mud off their hearts as well as their football boots.

Surely, the dirty old men weren't just a problem for girls like Lulu. Lulu has always known that when big people say, 'big boys don't cry', that this is completely wrong! Boys need to be allowed to cry. Big ones and little ones! They need people to want to listen to them too! Even if the boys don't seem to show it the same way as girls, and mightn't say very much at all.

Lulu really hopes they find a way to be the kind of man who could be kind and gentle as well as strong, and love themselves too.

It's never too late to begin.

# Big Brothers

So even though Lulu never really understood her five big brothers, or what their hearts were like, she thinks it's important now to at least say something about them all. That's because Lulu always did and always will love each and every one of them very, very much!

Lulu shines so much love out to them all, even now when one may just pass her on the street without wanting to even say hello. On those days, she knows and feels it is even more important to beam the love to them and say, "Hello in there, hello!"

# Oldest Brother

Oldest brother was very much older than Lulu indeed, and even though he really, really liked books the same as Daddy did, he had to leave school so he could learn how to run the pub like Daddy.

He got very sick when he was growing up. First thing Lulu or anyone else knew about it, was one night when the smaller ones were in bed, that Oldest Brother started coughing. Lulu remembers he was out standing on the first landing by the little gas heater and he coughed up lots of red, red blood!

This was very shocking.

Lulu doesn't remember what else happened that night, but he was taken to hospital and had to stay there for months and months and months. And on some Sunday afternoons, they were allowed to go with Mammy to see him, and on those days, he used to be sitting in a chair in this enormous big green house with plants inside and open windows in the big garden.

It might have only been a day or two after Oldest Brother coughed the blood up, that two men came to the house dressed in white suits and wearing white masks on their faces. They were like spacemen. The house was very quiet that day, and everyone seemed to be frightened.

They sprayed lots of stuff into Oldest Brother's bedroom and came to the kitchen to show Mammy how to deep clean all the plates, cups, knives and forks. After that, there were separate ones marked and kept, that only Oldest Brother could ever use. So even picking a knife and fork from the drawer became a scary business.

Lulu, Perfect Sister and Play Brother all had to go to hospital and get strange injections in their arms and then if the little needle marks got bumpy and itchy, they had to get a big injection in their arm. Lulu really didn't enjoy that, but it meant that they wouldn't get sick like Oldest Brother did.

He did come home eventually, but Lulu really knew even less about him after all that. Nowadays, so many years later, this old frail man passes Lulu in the street, with his hat hiding his eyes a lot, his collar up to keep out the cold and Lulu has to call out his name so he will come back, even for a moment, to say a little. Just enough for Lulu to pass some love to his big hidden heart.

I love you.

# Unknown Brother

Unknown Brother had lots of great big fat tablets that were kept in the cupboard in tins and he had to take these every day for months and months, so he wouldn't get as sick as Oldest Brother.

Apart from that, it's like Lulu never ever knew Unknown Brother at all, except that he and Far Away Brother used to fight each other all the time, every day it seemed. They really punched and hurt each other a lot, and they had to share a bedroom, next to the girls' big attic room. Sometimes, Mammy couldn't stop them fighting and had to threaten them with the dog's lead, and Lulu remembers one day at least when Daddy bounced their heads together to make them stop. Lulu feels the pain in her own head and especially her heart when she remembers this.

On some nights, when Unknown Brother and Far Away Brother slept in the bedroom next to our girls' room in the attic, they would be messing about fighting or play fighting.

If Daddy and Mammy had gone to bed already, Daddy would shout up for them to stop and warn them that he was going to come upstairs with the window pole! The window pole was to be feared. Much longer than Lulu and made of bright brown wood with a big brass hook on the end. No one would want to be hit with that.

So Daddy would rage up the stairs and as he would bash about with the pole on their bed, the boys would shout out, "Please Daddy! No! Aghh! Eghh!" All the while perfect Sister and Lulu held their breath, making sure Daddy wouldn't come in and hit them too, but he never did.

But, this would be the funniest, funniest thing. Instead of being terrible and horrible, when Daddy went away downstairs again, the boys would laugh and laugh and laugh. And they put on these big loud cries and yelps to make daddy think he was hurting them, but they weren't hurt, or weren't ever going to show it. And Perfect Sister and Lulu would laugh and laugh too, but quietly.

On nights like these, it was a great big winning feeling, because Daddy had been outwitted and the boys won!

But it's a very sad kind of missing piece of a jigsaw not really knowing Unknown Brother. And even though Lulu has tried to find ways to find the piece with him, it just has to sit like that jigsaw with a hole in it, and it's nobody's fault. It never is when a jigsaw piece gets lost.

# Contented Brother

Contented Brother stayed on at school like Unknown Brother did, what seemed like a very posh grammar school that the three biggest brothers all went to. He was the first one in the family to get a car after Daddy did.

Contented Brother went to work in a very important job too. It's odd how big people decide that some jobs are important and some just aren't. That can't be right and Lulu's sure God would agree with her.

Contented Brother was always so happy and thought everything was just a laugh, even the horrible stuff that happened to any of them, except him! Lulu wonders if that was mostly because Mammy seemed to love him so much. Or maybe Mammy loved him so much because he was always happy! Or maybe every one of them was always trying to work out if they were loved enough. We all have our own heart.

Maybe it was because he got to stay on at school and learn lots like geography and the weather that he always loved to talk about. Maybe he was very happy because he didn't have to go on to work in the pub!

Mammy always seemed to be very kind to him. Lulu remembers this and thinks she was probably jealous of him at times of the year like his birthday. Contented Brother and Lulu's birthdays were only four days apart. Lulu's first, then Contented Brother's.

When it was Contented Brother's birthday, Mammy would give Lulu money to run down to the wee shop to buy him a little birthday cake for when he came home from work. Little, with icing and a cherry on top, but still, a cake! And he was all grown up and didn't need a cake as much as someone much younger.

Now, Lulu really doesn't remember if a cake was ever bought for her birthday, no matter how hard she wracks her brain to remember that. Though she did get the best birthday present ever the year mammy somehow bought her her most prized Jacko roller skates.

Jacko skates with red leather straps and wheels of rubber with beautiful shiny ball bearings inside. Jacko skates that meant you could fly down all the streets and alleys with bumpy cracks or smooth, smooth flagstones. Jacko skates that made Lulu feel she could fly. Jacko skates that were the next best thing to a bike.

Lulu only remembers when she turned thirteen and because she was a teenager, Mammy paid for a cake and Lulu was allowed to bring two friends into the sitting room for a little tea party, which Lulu got ready herself. But those stories are for another book when Lulu was trying to grow up and became 'Noodles'.

# Far Away Brother

He always seemed very strange to Lulu. She knows now that it was easier to think he was strange, rather than just feel how she felt like she couldn't understand him. Probably no one in the family ever understood him, and maybe that's why he sort of disappeared. Somehow, he never really seemed to be there, even when he was in the same room. And he always got picked on a lot.

Lulu never could understand that when he got his bit of pay, after he started work at the pub after school, and went and bought all the best comics, that he would sit on them all and take out one at a time to read. Then, when he had finished, he would burn them all in the fire. What could possibly have made him need to do that when there were at least three of them younger than him who really, really wanted to read them too? And he used to pick his nose all the time when he was reading them! Maybe this was a good way to get them to go away and leave him alone, and it worked!

Lulu thinks now, that he just really, really needed to know that his own things were precious and private to him, and somehow, he just needed to make himself disappear a lot.

Lulu does know that Far Away Brother got it very hard from Daddy because he was left-handed and for some stupid, horrible reason, he was made to eat with his knife and fork like someone right-handed, at Sunday dinner time. Can you even imagine trying to do that, without spilling your food, or getting really tight and angry inside? Or getting blamed?

Going far, far away into yourself is probably a really good way of escaping, but you can get lost in there.

One wonderful thing Far Away Brother could do was play the mouth organ. Now all these years later, Lulu is so very relieved to know he taught himself how to do that. If the feelings he got when he played are anything like as happy and soothing as they were for Lulu when they were all in bed at night, then Lulu knows he could know love inside his own heart and forget the bad stuff.

# Play Brother

Play Brother was the youngest brother and one up from Lulu, so they spent a lot of time together playing and fighting. They shared the same big bed in Mammy and Daddy's room when they were very little. Well, that was up until the whole ceiling fell down on top of Lulu when she was sick in bed one time, and after that, she got moved to the big attic girls' room.

At night, before the older ones were sent to bed, Lulu and Play Brother used to play their favourite game together. He had a torch he got for Christmas and he kept it under his pillow and they shared a tiny little plastic toy. It was a yellow little horse with a rider on top and when you pulled it along on a string, the little plastic horse's legs would move, as if to trot. This tiny little toy was small enough to fit inside their hands.

When the light was put out and Mammy had said prayers with them and gone downstairs, out would come the torch and the yellow horse. When they put their knees up and their legs in funny positions, the blankets looked like big mountains and deep, deep valleys. And when the torch lit it all, it was like a completely magical land somewhere far, far away. They were cowboys and Indians, German soldiers, and the three wise men. Everything in the whole world they wanted to be in those magical lands of their knees.

And they would sing The Whistling Gypsy, as Play Brother moved the torch to light different parts as they gently pulled the horse along in this magical adventure.

*'The whistling gypsy came over the hill, down through the valley so shady, and he whistled and he sang till the green woods rang, and he won the heart of a lay-a-a-dy!'*

In those magical adventures, they could be anyone, anywhere they wanted to, and it was a joyful world!

Lulu thinks Play Brother never felt safe enough to be himself at home. And this came true on the day his first-year big school report came home, or didn't come home! Whatever happened, Play Brother was afraid to let his report come home because he knew it wasn't going to be a good one, and so, he threw it away or something.

But Daddy found out somehow, and on that Saturday morning, Lulu remembers Daddy came upstairs and dragged Play Brother out of bed and out the back to beat him with a stick!

Now why did he have to do that? And what could ever possibly be that bad that you have to get beaten for it? Lulu will never be able to understand that and can still see in her brothers now grown-up eyes, how very, very much this whole thing hurt him and changed him, as if it just isn't safe to ever let anybody know what you really feel inside.

What happens to a lovely heart when bad things like that are done to it? And how do we fix it? Maybe we have to get very, very, very good at taking ourselves to a magical land that we create all for ourselves inside, and soak up all the love in that. If we don't, then those old cuts and scars just keep opening up again and again, every time we are scared or hurt.

Scared and scarred are nearly the same word!

Love is inside us and that's who we are really. Underneath all the bruises, and bumps and, cuts and scars. Love is really the only medicine. Medicine that tastes nice and makes us better.

# Robin Hood

Lulu prefers to remember Play Brother, Perfect Sister and her, playing 'Robin Hood and his Merry Men', as they ran down the back entry, along the bottom and back up the avenue to home.

All in their glory on their make believe wonderful white horses and with their school coats tied around the neck but the arms free, like great capes of gold and yellow, and green and red, and singing 'Robin Hood'. The only bit Lulu didn't like was that Perfect Sister of course was Maid Marian and Play Brother was always Robin Hood while Lulu was always, always Friar Tuck!

> *'Robin Hood, Robin Hood, riding through the glen,*
> *Robin Hood, Robin Hood with his merry men.*
> *Feared by the bad, loved by the good!*
> *Robin Hood Robin Hood. Robin Hood.'*

This magical world!

# Robin Hood Spoiled

One bad day, the magic of their Robin Hood adventures was turned all wrong, sad and difficult. It's very hard to not let this bad day mess up the wonder, joy and freedom of their Robin Hood adventures!

There were loose stones outside our garage out the back. And sometimes, the drain there would get blocked, fill up and overflow with all the toilet sewage. It was really not nice and was very smelly.

On this one day, when they came running up to home after they had sorted out all the baddies and saved all the goodies in their adventure, Daddy called them in and lined them up in the kitchen. He was very angry and wanted to know which one of them had kicked stones down the drain and made it overflow.

"It wasn't us, Daddy!"

"It wasn't me, Daddy!"

This was all they could say, and they were all very scared. Daddy didn't like that answer and got angrier and angrier. Sooner or later, he exploded and slapped one of them hard on the face!

Now the strange thing is, memories are strange because Lulu can't remember which one of them got slapped. But Lulu feels like it was her, and probably the others would feel that too, because watching it, fearing it, feeling it and hearing it would have been as real for each of them, no matter which one did actually get slapped.

Lulu can hear the slap, feel the stinging burning on her face and can see them all kind of frozen, like when a film gets stuck in one place. Lulu still wonders how Daddy himself must have felt when he remembered doing it and seeing all those sad frightened eyes looking back at him. Or if he even did remember.

The amazing thing is, Biggest Sister was in the kitchen and she decided to stand up for them that day! She shouted back at Daddy that he was doing a very bad thing and that he shouldn't be like this with them. She was very sad, very upset, very angry and brave enough to stand up and say what they weren't able to say! And she did it for Lulu and for all of them! She was the first person ever to stand up to Daddy and tell him he was wrong!

What an amazing big-hearted thing to do for your wee brother and sisters.

Biggest Sister decided to leave home to go and live in Belfast soon after that day. She probably had to get away to be able to feel what she was feeling and find a way to feel free! Like nearly every one of us did eventually.

Nothing else happened that day.

So now, Lulu has decided to bring back the magic, colours and horses of Robin Hood with all the wonderful feelings from that day and make them so very big in her heart that the bad parts change shape and fade away. Even though that is sometimes difficult and needs some work, it's worth it.

# Big and Kind People

Lulu was very, very lucky that a few big grown-up people found her, or she found them, and they gave her so much love and kindness and made her feel very special inside.

When she thinks of them now, Lulu feels so much joy and happiness bursting out from her heart, enough to love the whole world. And that's just how our big hearts are meant to shine!

Lulu is so excited right now that she can hardly write at all, but really, really wants you to know that there are always people just down the street or even somewhere far away, who make it their business to polish up your heart, and their own at the same time. And they often don't even know they are doing it! Perhaps we just have to knock on their door and not run away, and say hello!

## Mr McCarthy

Mr McCarthy lived at number 8, and he was a very kind man. Always and forever kind to Lulu. He lived with his lovely wife though Lulu never really got to know her because Lulu spent most of the time in Mr McCarthy's lovely little garden or watching him work in his little shed with the big wood turning machine.

Somehow, Lulu doesn't know how she started to go into Mr McCarthy's garden with Play Brother, and asked him if she could help him cut the grass.

Lulu's family only had a tiny little patch of grass at their front door and he seemed to have the most beautiful garden with a really long strip of grass and flowers growing up all along the edges. No one could have guessed the magical place waiting behind the old wooden tall gate, when outside, there was just an old entry alley that was grey and dull.

His grass was always perfectly cut and he had a funny old lawnmower that turned its blades as you pushed it along. He had a pair of proper garden shears that he polished up in his work shed so the blades could stay sharp. Lulu only needed scissors for their little square of grass and that was good enough.

Mr McCarthy allowed Lulu and Play Brother, to come in for a while and cut the grass for him. Sometimes, Lulu would ring their front bell to ask if his grass needed any cutting. And even though a lot of the time his grass didn't really need cutting again, Mr McCarthy always allowed them to come into his garden.

Sometimes, he gave Lulu and Play Brother a thruppence for doing such a fine job, though probably they didn't do it as well as he could. But he seemed to always say yes.

It's just such a simple enormous word…YES!

Some days, he would let them take out his two wooden deckchairs to just play and sit as they tried to work out how to put them up the right way round. Lulu never could get that right, because they were so big and confusing. But it didn't matter.

Mr McCarthy's little shed was a very special place and he made beautiful wooden lamps, boxes, bowls and things. She would stand for hours watching him turn the big machine with his hands and Lulu would tidy up by sweeping all the dust and wood chips off his very old worn worktable. He had so many tools all hung on nails alongside the back wall and you could see out across his garden as we worked.

Lulu always felt peaceful and happy there, even though Mr. McCarthy was very old and she was very little. Maybe that's because he didn't have any children of his own, and maybe he just liked Lulu's company. Lulu doesn't remember them talking about anything in particular but they didn't need to.

Lulu knows she was just as special to Mr McCarthy as he was to her because once, on her birthday, Mrs McCarthy came out from her kitchen door and gave Lulu a box of chocolates. It was a beautiful box called 'Weekend'.

Lulu couldn't believe that anyone would ever give her a whole box of chocolates still wrapped up in plastic. This was very, very special indeed. Now, Lulu must confess that she didn't actually like the sweets much inside, but she ate them all anyway because this was such a special gift!

Another time, Mr McCarthy gave Lulu one of his beautiful big tall wooden lamps, though Lulu never really knew what to do with that, but Mammy kept it beside her bed for years and years and years.

Maybe Mr McCarthy knew Lulu just needed a special place to go, and where she could just be herself. And maybe, Mr McCarthy felt special because Lulu wanted to spend time with him while he worked.

He was such a lovely kind man and it makes Lulu's heart sing now as she remembers him.

## Miss O'Toole

Miss O'Toole - a beautiful thin lady with white hair and pearls around her neck and she was Lulus teacher for a whole year in P3.

She was very kind and let the class sing a lot and learn new songs like 'The Minstrel Boy' and 'The Foggy Dew'! Lulu used to love going home to sing them to Mammy who always knew the words too!

Miss O'Toole was very kind to Lulu and sometimes invited her and a boy called Paul to go to her house after school to sing.

They would knock her big blue door and when she opened, she brought them in to her front sitting room and they would take turns to stand up and sing a song for her. When they had all finished, she always gave them tea and buns, and biscuits. It was kind of a proud feeling.

Lulu just loved Miss O'Toole and definitely knew what it was like to feel specially loved just for singing songs. Lulu doesn't think Miss O'Toole could possibly know how wonderful it felt and has always felt ever since, to have someone love you just for being yourself!

And Lulu has always loved to sing ever since!

# Primary School

Lulu remembers wetting herself on her first day, standing by a little wooden easel and asked to paint a picture. Not a good start!

The little wooden desks with inkwells and benches attached, had chewing gum stuck underneath by many little ones before her, and you could pick away at the old rock-hard goo instead of listening to the teacher.

Little bottles of milk were delivered to the gates every morning. In winter, when the frost was hard, the bottles would be frozen and one or two boys would carry them into the classroom to set before the open fire. As they melted, the milk separated into yellowy sour tops and thick white bottoms. Still they had to drink it. Boke!

Teachers who loved to sing taught them all the old rebel songs and songs of Ireland.

Cruel teachers who loved their canes or leather straps and seemed to itch to use it if anyone did anything wrong. Just to hit little children! Lulu didn't get slapped more than once she can remember. But she watched many who did, and she was very afraid and is certain that nothing could have been bold enough to need to be hit, sometimes until the blood came.

One teacher, Mr Smith, was just plain cruel. He sellotaped two rulers together and hit people, mostly the boys, with the edges up, so the wood would nip at the same time. Everyone hated him, but mostly underneath that was the fear and dread.

That's usually where fear is hidden…underneath.

He liked to stand behind his big desk with his bottom covering all the heat from the coal fire, so none of the little ones could get warm.

Once, he sent Lulu up the street to the main school building to get a long weight from another teacher. What a strange errand. Well, it seemed many hours later when she came back to the classroom empty handed, everybody laughed and laughed. Everybody except Lulu, who was just totally confused.

It's so easy to make fun of little children... no matter how old. Even little children still wanting love inside their big grown up bodies.

Lulu remembers the lovely Nature study homework, where they had to collect lots of things from outside. On that very special sunny evening, Lulu sneaked into the big secondary school grounds and spent hours wandering in joy through all the different trees. No one else was around, just the birdsong, and she collected so many different leaves and twigs, with all the colours, shapes and smells.

This was what peace and joy feels like.

And she has remembered the names of all those leaves and trees ever since.

Break times.

A mass of children making noise and managing to play a whole list of games all at once, and somehow found a room for it all. Releasing and letting go all the tight control of the classroom.

A good long skipping rope was a fine prize indeed, ensuring many friends to join in. A ball or even better, two and a little spare patch of wall to master the new skill and the rhymes to go with it, and walking home for lunch singing and rehearsing the latest new song to be ready to sing to Mammy. And she usually knew them all.

Mr Green, a kind and gentle man, made Lulu's last year at primary school really special. Winning the three pence prize for being the best speller in the class was like winning the world. That feeling of pride and delight in her heart has never left. And she has always been a brilliant speller, ever since then. Isn't that funny?

But then...

# Mr Delaney

Mr Delaney was the headmaster. He was short and round with dark hair and round spectacles. And he smoked a pipe! He was very important! He was of course, also scary because no one ever wanted to be sent to his office and he had a very big cane, that Lulu thankfully never felt the pain of.

Mr Delaney also knew Daddy and Mammy very well because he went to their pub. Every week on a Monday, all the children brought pennies in for the black babies in Africa and the pennies had to be counted. Mr Delaney took all the pennies from each classroom to his room to count.

One day, he gave Lulu the most important job to do for him. Nothing as important had ever been asked of Lulu before.

When she went to his office, he had all the pennies set out in little stacks. Then he counted the stacks into little bags. Each week, he asked a pupil to take the pennies out of school and along to the little corner shop to get them changed into pound notes!

A very important job indeed!

Delighted and excited about this job, Lulu set out, so desperate to get everything right. As Lulu ran—she was always running—along past the school gates, she tripped and the whole bag of pennies spilled all over the road.

Oh, No! Oh, no! Oh, No!

Praying all the time that no one would see her, Lulu desperately gathered up every penny she could find and searched quickly to make sure none had got lost down the drain. But she knew she had to get back to school quickly.

Lulu decided to go to the corner shop, but disaster struck, there were pennies missing and the shopkeeper couldn't give her pound notes because the money didn't add up anymore.

Lulu was too terrified to dare tell Mr Delaney what had happened to her, because she decided that he just wouldn't believe what really happened. Then, he would be bound to believe Lulu had stolen some of the money. Lulu was frantic and couldn't imagine any of it, because she certainly wouldn't ever steal but completely believed he would think she had. Then, there would be big trouble!

What was Lulu to do? What would you do?

So, because anything was better than being thought of as a thief, Lulu went into Mr Delaney to explain that the shopkeeper said he didn't count the money correctly and it was short, so she couldn't change it all into notes.

Lulu has to catch her breath even now as she remembers saying this! How could she possibly be strong enough to stand in front of Mr Delaney in his big office, and tell him a lie? How was telling that lie ever going to be better than just saying what did happen? But Lulu totally believed she could not just tell the truth. Mr Delaney didn't say very much. Or Lulu doesn't remember what he did say. He just took the penny bags back and Lulu went back to class. The whole thing was never mentioned again.

Lulu still doesn't know if Mr Delaney believed her, or if he thought she had stolen from him and the black babies!

Did he tell her Daddy what happened? Well that can't have been true. Did he believe she was a thief? That can't have been true. Or could it? And surely, he didn't believe that he added it all up wrong himself.

Lulu will never know. But Lulu is sure now, that Mr Delaney wouldn't have believed what she did tell him.

He never asked Lulu to do that special job again, but she is still really relieved to know that no more was ever said about it, at least not to her!

The only way Lulu can make sense of her decision that day, was that somewhere along the line, she had decided that if something wrong had happened then you just couldn't risk telling the whole truth. Because? Because you just wouldn't be believed, and something very bad was going to happen. And Lulu had lots of evidence for that at home.

And that's how secrets get stuck inside us. When we are afraid of what other people will do with what we tell them. That we will get hurt one way or another, and feel bad about ourselves even more.

Secrets have a way of getting heavier and heavier in our hearts, no matter how big we become.

# Bedtimes

Lulu got moved to sleep in the attic with all the sisters after the ceiling fell in on Lulu when she was sick one time in the bed in Mammy and Daddy's bedroom. No one knows how it happened, but all of a sudden, all of the ceiling, the cement and the wooden floorboards came down right on top of Lulu in the bed! There was a lot of dust and dirt, but somehow, Lulu never got hurt! God was there again!

Anyway, this meant that bedtimes got special and exciting. Perfect Sister and Lulu went to bed a lot earlier than the big, big ones and Far Away Brother slept in the back attic next door.

Perfect Sister was good at tricking Lulu when the light had to be put out. They agreed that they would take it in turns to get out of bed, across the floor to the switch and then back again. Lulu hated the dark and the wallpaper always made strange ugly scary faces when the light was out and there was just light from the street outside.

She hated being up there alone if it wasn't during the daylight. But every time it was Perfect Sister's turn and Lulu was all snuggled up safe in bed, Perfect Sister would say Lulu had to do it. She was very good at just staying in bed and sitting it out until Lulu had to give in and make the dangerous journey back across the bedroom floor.

Some nights when they were still awake and Far Away Brother came to bed, he would play his mouth organ in the dark. He made such beautiful sounds and songs, and he played along when Perfect Sister would sing her favourite 'Santa Lucia'.

*'Somewhere a distant shore moonlight is beaming*
*There on the water my boat lies sleeping*
*Softly a serenade whispers I love you Santa Lucia Santa Lucia.'*

Or she sang '*Plaisir D'amour*' which means the joys of love, because she was learning French at big school. Lulu always felt so safe and, happy and full of love when they made the music together before going to sleep. And on other nights, they all sang:

*'There's a hole in my bucket,*
*dear Liza, dear Liza.'*

And they all laughed and laughed.

Singing all their cares away, clearing the shadows in the wallpaper and everywhere else, lullabies to soothe and fill their hearts.

Lulu's heart is very full of love now. All the shadows have been turned to light.

Night, night everyone…

Make sure you fill your heart with loving lullabies tonight and dream.

I love you, and a special love to all my brothers and sisters.

THE END…

or maybe

it's the BEGINNING…